A Higher Channel

Conversations with Higher Spirits about Everyday Life

Alavan

Copyright © 2024

All rights reserved.

No part of this book may be reproduced or transmitted in any form or by any means, electronic or mechanical, including photocopying, recording, or by any information storage and retrieval system, without written permission from the author, except for the inclusion of brief quotations in a review.

Contact: ahigherchannel.org

Introduction

My life has been unbelievable. It is what brought me to write this book. I have been a spiritual and wellness junkie for years and was not prepared for all that I experienced. The following introduction to the book was provided by a higher spirit that I would talk to hundreds of times over many years. His suggestion for my opening:

"I am and have been the recipient of the most elaborate and exceptional experience, and with what follows, you may think this is unreal, but I tell you that my life has been unreal. I was offered the gift of Spirit to come into my life for me to show you what Spirit can do." – Botra

This book is dedicated to Somé, with whom I experienced Spirit, never-ending joy, and love for over thirty years.

The Beginning, Spring, 1990

Somé, Paige, and I sat on our bed for a meditation and sound toning session. Somé was new to this, although Paige and I had studied spirituality for years. We had just returned from a Sedona retreat where we learned new techniques for this type of meditation. We began softly toning with our voices, alternating sounds at higher pitches. Somé closed his eyes and lowered his head. I suggested we all picture a tunnel of light as we began the meditation. The last time we did this, Somé fell asleep, but this time was different.

The room was lit with candles, and we were toning softly when, suddenly, his head jerked up, and his eyes opened wide. Even though we were sitting in a circle, he wasn't looking at Paige or me. He started slowly scanning the room like he'd never seen before. His face showed complete surprise and unfamiliarity. As his gaze came back toward us, I asked, "Who are you?

Whoever was in his consciousness locked his gaze on me and asked, "Who are YOU?"

"Alavan," I said. His head jerked a little, his eyes widened, and his body looked ready to lunge. Not knowing what to do, I shouted, "Spirit, protect us!" We both started toning loudly to break the moment's energy as best we could. Somé's eyes closed, and his head slowly lowered. I looked at Paige with wide eyes as if to say, "What just happened?" She looked startled, too, and we continued toning, slowly reducing the volume, until he woke up a few minutes later.

We asked him if he remembered anything. He said he just visualized the tunnel, and that's the last thing he could recall. I believed I knew what was happening and explained that it seemed like he channeled a spirit that knew who I was and saw me as a threat. The spirit didn't know what was happening or why he was there and looked ready to defend himself at all costs. However, the good news was that a governing spirit or group of spirits knew what was happening and guided the experience so that no actual harm was done. I mean, what if Somé never came back? What if that spirit got trapped in his body forever? I was not prepared to answer or deal with these questions at the time.

I believe the experience opened a doorway for him. After that, Somé said he started to hear voices—lots of them. It was his first channeling experience in what would become a regular occurrence.

Table of Contents

Introduction 1

The Beginning, Spring, 1990 2

Chapter 1: Upheaval In Monterey 5

Chapter 2: The Walk-Ins 16

Chapter 3: Meeting The Walk-Ins 29

Chapter 4: An Unexpected Breakthrough 41

Chapter 5: Zitron 53

Chapter 6: Giving Up All Emotion 68

Chapter 7: New Beginnings 86

Chapter 8: Guests Arrive 113

Chapter 9: Dimensions 130

Chapter 10: Energy Portals 138

Chapter 11: Are Those Stars? 150

Chapter 12: Healing Energy and Helping Others 162

Chapter 13: A Mother's Pride 175

Chapter 14: Disgruntled employee 186

Chapter 15: Aloha 201

Chapter 16: The Final Journey 218

Bibliography 223

Chapter 1: Upheaval In Monterey

Let's back up a bit. My name is Alavan. I didn't get that name at birth, but I changed it in the '90s during a significant period of change.

I left Denver for Monterey, California, in the winter of 1988 because my mom lived there and was willing to take me in. My brother had also moved there a couple of years earlier. My mom lived in a two-bedroom apartment near the old Fisherman's Wharf and gave me one of the rooms to help me settle in. I remember getting a cheap 10-speed bicycle and riding the recreation trail along the coast to Cannery Row, where there were many restaurants and the famous Monterey Aquarium.

I found work as a busser at the same upscale seafood restaurant where my brother worked. Of course, he gave me a good recommendation. The restaurant work was busy, and the money was decent, but I felt unfulfilled. I wanted more out of life. I did not know what I wanted, but I knew working at a restaurant wasn't it.

I frequented a health food store just down the street from the restaurant. It was small but had all the usual goodies: vitamins, bulk grains, groceries, and produce. It also had a magazine rack at the front of the store with flyers and advertisements for local events. I talked to one of the workers there and asked how they liked their job. They said they loved it because it represented many of their personal philosophies: sustainability, organic food, and giving back to the community. These values aligned with mine since I had been a vegetarian for a couple of years. I applied and got a job in the grocery department. I was very excited!

Everyone was super nice at the store. I was tasked with learning the store layout and where everything was located. It wasn't a huge store: vitamins on the right, groceries in the middle, dairy and refrigeration in the back, and produce and bulk items on the left. In the produce section, I met Somé, the man with whom I would embark on the most amazing journey of my life and spend the next 32 years.

Somé was a consultant hired to improve the produce department, as he had done for many other independent stores. He had experience in commercial groceries, especially produce, and a talent for setting up beautiful displays. I was assigned to work with him, and he taught me everything about produce display, rotation, and ordering.

Since we worked together, we often went to lunch and talked about our lives. I learned he had been married for 30 years, had 5 kids, and had a couple of grandchildren. He also told me he was gay and had known since early childhood. The 1950s were tough for being gay, and very few came out during those times. His brother, Ernie, was also gay and advised him to "find a girl and marry her – there's no other way." He loved his family but wanted to change his life and expand his experiences.

We both had challenging childhoods, but Somé's was much harder. His mother handed over the care of her five children to her sister, who raised them with her child. They grew up on an orchard in San Mateo

County, California, in the 1940s and 1950s. They were made to work on the orchard from as early as five years old. Their aunt kept a ledger of the debts they accumulated and the money they earned. There was also rampant sexual abuse in the household. The aunt's child was favored and received better meals and treatment. It was an authoritarian environment without love, support, or genuine affection.

My mom raised my brother and me by herself and modeled a good work ethic, relying only on her high school diploma. We moved from Idaho to Nevada and settled in central California in the 1970s. I don't remember much about my childhood, but I have fond memories of visiting my grandparents in Idaho at Christmas and swimming in the Cascade Mountains in the summer.

As Somé began his personal transformation, the next few months were a whirlwind. In September 1989, with his children grown, he left his wife and home in Santa Cruz and found a small studio cottage near the health food store where we worked. About a month later, he moved to Seaside (just north of Monterey) and then a bit further north to Watsonville.

Then, on October 17th, 1989, the Loma Prieta earthquake hit the Bay Area, disrupting the World Series in San Francisco and shaking the streets in Monterey. I remember the power being out in the store just outside Monterey, and groceries had fallen off the shelves. The earthquake was scary, but the aftershocks were even more unsettling, making it hard to sleep. Power and water were restored over the next few days, but the impact was felt for years in the Bay Area.

I remember finding a local couple conducting "Peaceful Warrior" workshops based on the book. I attended one for a few days. The workshops focused on paying attention to details and finding light and joy in everything we do. I enjoyed exploring that part of myself that is connected to the universe and everyone else.

In the final months of 1989, Somé and I got to know each other better and kept finding new ways to improve ourselves. One of the store owners gave Somé some audio cassettes from Dr. Wayne Dyer, a great author and motivational speaker. It was probably the first time Somé experienced self-reflection and self-awareness from an outside source. This was just the beginning of a whirlwind journey for both of us.

Fast forward to a six-hour channeling session in San Francisco in the mid-1990s. Somé is sitting in a wicker chair in the small dining area of our one-bedroom apartment. You can sometimes hear the refrigerator behind him cycling while Kitaro music plays in the background. Four cigarettes are lined up in front of him on a turquoise Hawaiian print placemat with a Zippo lighter beside them. A ceramic coffee mug and ashtray are also on the glass table. He sits with his elbows on the table, hands clasped, fingers intertwined, touching his mouth as he gently leans forward into them.

He has begun channeling a higher spirit, the higher spirit of our friend Brent, who recently ended a relationship with my brother, Alisal. Brent is struggling with the breakup and wondering what his next steps should be. Somé offered to channel his higher spirit, Montaviel.

He has channeled his own spirits before but never someone else's. He sits with his hands clasped, rubs them together, and in his mind, he starts to separate himself after talking to Spirit to prepare for the session. He says that as he gets close, he feels an energetic pull as he prepares to "step aside" for another spirit to enter his body. He separates his hands and moves them back and forth as if feeling the energy between them. Then he relaxes his arms and leans back a little into the chair. He has one hand clasped in front of his mouth. His head starts moving slowly from side to side, and then his hand drops slowly to the table, his forearm resting on it. He bows his head, and his lips seem to mumble something. As he slowly raises his head, his abdomen rolls up slightly, indicating the arrival of new energy and Somé stepping aside. His head slowly shakes, and his fingers open and close as Montaviel gets his bearings. It takes a few minutes for him to settle in and get up to speed. He shakes his head slowly, raises and lowers his brow, opens his eyes, looks around, then at us, and a warm smile emerges.

Alavan was relieved to see Montaviel. "You made it!"

Montaviel responded philosophically: " It seems like we always make it one way or another. We are part of an everlasting experience that never ends and a new one that never stops beginning," he said with a smile.

Alavan asked, "How does it feel to be back in form?"

"It feels very different," Montaviel admitted, "because of who he is and the difficulties he's experiencing (referring to Brent). But nonetheless, we're here," he said, glancing at Brent, "and we're here for you."

Montaviel continued, "So, as our ongoing newcomer, we have a new experience unfolding. It may not be unfolding as you planned, but it's unfolding, nonetheless. We can start wherever you want."

Brent was thoughtful. "I sort of planned on starting chronologically. It's been about a year since I was first introduced to the concept of past lives. I want to know if there's anything significant about my past lives that affects who I am now."

"All of it," Montaviel said simply.

Brent then shifted the topic to something more personal. "Can you tell me anything about my blood parents, who gave me up for adoption? Maybe why?"

"To whom are you referring? Which one?" Montaviel inquired.

"My father, my stepfather," Brent clarified.

"I think Somé covered it pretty well during our recent discussion," Montaviel recalled. "The reasons behind what happened aren't there to understand. The events transpired because of many realities at that time. Your blood father, as you call him, is your grandfather. Your mother was an acquaintance of his. He chose not to be a part of anything. Every part of your existence in this life was well planned and prepared."

Brent pressed on about another sensitive topic. "My adoptive parents never talked about why they couldn't have children. Is there anything I need to know about that?"

"No," Montaviel responded.

Brent, referencing his readings, said, "Bradshaw talks about focusing on each parent's influence on my life. Can you give me more insight on my mom since she's the one I have the hardest time with? Maybe there are things I've blocked out?"

"What you know and what you perceive you know are completely opposite," Montaviel explained. "What you perceive your mother to be in your reality is one way. What she actually is in another reality is completely different."

Montaviel then addressed Brent's overall understanding, "Are you forming an opinion based on emotion because you want something to be there that isn't? Or is it because of a fantasy for many different reasons? Most of all, what you feel is a direct connection to what you want to feel. It's not actually real as what we want to call real. It's all part of an experience, anyway. And the experience doesn't hold what you want it to hold. The experience is the experience. What you want to feel is what you want to feel. Don't confuse the two. They have nothing to do with each other."

Brent acknowledged this, pondering if it applied to both parents.

"I know what you're thinking, and I know the question you want to place out there and you're kind of going around it," Montaviel noted. "You're going around what you really want to know."

Brent asked, "Okay, was I abused as a child?"

"What do you consider abuse?" Montaviel questioned.

Brent hesitated. "Well, physical or mental abuse. Am I blocking any of that out?"

"There was no physical abuse," Montaviel clarified. " Mental abuse is to one's reality of what mental abuse is. Mental abuse to one person can be angst and anxiety. And it can be anything. But I don't want to mislead you and I don't want you to mislead yourself as to what you contribute to mental abuse. The mental abuse that you consider in your own reality base to be mental abuse was there in a significant form. What I see is not what you see. What I see is part of the experience. What you see is a way to justify why you do what you do now, which actually has no bearing or significance."

Brent then asked about his emotions, noticing a difference between himself and his family. "Where do I get my emotions from? Is there a reason I feel so different?"

"It's yours. Embrace it. It's you. There's nothing wrong with it. It enhances what you do and every part of your thoughts. Embrace that. It's you," Montaviel encouraged with a smile.

Lastly, Brent mentioned a coworker, Kristen, "There's a girl at work, Kristen, who I feel is strongly attracted to me. I am attracted to her sexually but not romantically. I don't know if it's because of Alisal being in my life or if it's something I need to experience."

"Why are you placing so many faces on one feeling?" Montaviel challenged. "Emotion has no face. Love has no face. Feeling has no face. It's all an experience. When you start assigning faces to each feeling, you become the god and giver of your own destiny."

"The experience you feel should have no face. The love you feel should have no face. Placing a face on it doesn't help and will never become part of your wholeness."

"So, asking why something happens is like asking why this feeling has a different face. Why does one feeling have a female face and another a male face? Love has no face. Emotion has no face."

Brent remembered a recent decision and its impact. "When I decided to take that computer from Alisal, did I go against something beautiful in myself? I still feel a lot of guilt about it."

Montaviel chuckled, "If you wanted to, you could wake up in the morning, comb your hair the wrong way, and feel guilty about it."

Brent laughed and responded. "Okay, okay."

"What you do and how you do it has nothing to do with who you really are. Nothing." Montaviel continued. "A fleeting glance, a look the wrong way, a word – they're all the same. What you did, what you didn't do, how you did it, how you felt – none of it defines you. It's part of the feeling you wanted to create at that moment. For some reason, you felt you needed to create more feelings. You don't. You have enough. But you want to twist it, turn it, make it fit your face, not the face it belongs to."

Brent had another concern. "This comes from my upbringing in the Mormon religion. Am I keeping my body okay for my spirit with my drinking and smoking, or does it matter?"

Montaviel smiled warmly. "How much less does the beggar and drunk on the street have within themselves compared to you? How much more do you see yourself having? Every one of us is identical. Don't let one person's beliefs block you from accepting your wholeness. It's in all of us. We all have the same soul, the same spirit.

A Higher Channel

"What you do to enjoy life – drink, smoke, swear – it's all part of the experience. It has nothing to do with your wholeness. It doesn't bring you closer or take you further away from yourself. It never can and never will. It's a misconception that wholeness and spirituality are housed in a building with fancy things and dictated by one person's feelings. Why should we all feel like one person? We are many people, many beings, and every one of us is as pure as anyone else. What we do has no bearing on who we are. Don't look at what people do. Look at who we are. You can't see or feel it from someone else, but you know it's there. That's the beauty of all this."

Chapter 2: The Walk-Ins

A particular newsletter caught my eye while looking at the periodical stand in front of the health food store in the fall of 1989. The title was Light Speed, with the subtitle An Extraterrestrial Visionary Vehicle. I've always been cautious about spiritual content, so I was wary about what I was about to read. The articles mentioned that acceleration was unfolding on our planet. Vibrational energy was increasing, leading to many changes. People would feel less comfortable with the status quo, begin to recognize their light and wholeness and seek out environments and people who honor them. There would also be walk-ins and the authors of this newsletter were walk-ins.

What are walk-ins? According to them, "a 'walk-in' is a term used to describe a process in which a spirit that is inhabiting a body leaves, and a different spirit comes in" (Silarra and Savizar 1989, 123). This is for an extended period, unlike channeling. Channeling involves spirit displacement where your spirit moves aside so another spirit can reside in your mind or body. Channeling sessions can last from minutes to hours, but not usually more than a few hours due to the energetic toll on the body. Walk-ins are a complete substitution of the original spirit/soul of the body, done with full permission of the original spirit.

Their book, Conscious Channeling, explains two types of channeling: trance channeling and conscious channeling. Trance channeling involves completely giving over your body and consciousness to another entity. You are not aware of what is being said through you when it happens and generally do not remember anything when you come out of the trance state. Conscious channeling can involve a light trance state, but you are completely aware of everything as it happens through you. Your consciousness simply moves into the background and lets others into the foreground.

The authors prefer conscious channeling for a couple of reasons. One is that they are too "nosy" to miss out on the higher truth that comes through the entities that channel through them. They also mention that those interested in channeling for personal gain wouldn't attract many higher-dimensional spirits. "Spiritual ambition is only attractive to lower vibrational entities seeking power and recognition" (Savizar and Silarra 1989, 4).

If you genuinely desire to be a divine instrument for higher truth, love, and light simply because it allows you to experience the ecstasy and fulfillment of expressing your divinity in service to the Divine Plan, you might attract some incredible beings, including your own higher aspects.

The co-creation of Heaven on Earth is about bringing energy and information from other dimensions (Heaven) to Earth. One of the most exciting and beautiful ways to do this is by "saying 'yes' to our own divine spirits and making ourselves available to fifth-dimensional and above energies and entities as a divine instrument through which they can play" (Savizar and Silarra 1989, 4).

They talked about creating heaven on earth, but not in a religious way. To quote their newsletter, Light Speed, "Our version of the co-creation of Heaven on Earth is simple: You follow your own Divine Spirit without hesitation. Since all Divine Spirits are aligned with their part in the Divine Plan, you are always in the right place at the right time doing the right things with the right people. Life can't get much simpler. You don't even have to figure any of it out ahead of time" (Light Speed, issue three). They emphasized being free to express yourself without having your will imposed upon you by anything outside yourself and honoring that everyone else has that same right. Their motto is, "Follow your Spirit without hesitation," which I would come to know as "follow your first thought."

I was intrigued. I didn't see any red flags in what they were saying and, in fact, loved the content. It was genuine, direct, filled with divinity, love, hope, and an understanding that spans many dimensional realities. I wanted more.

What I liked about channeling was that you get information directly from a source. It's not filtered or interpreted by someone else. There's always some context, but the information has a certain purity that I find appealing. The spirits even gave me a nickname, "Mr. Information," because I asked so many questions. Believe it or not, they also have a good sense of humor!

A Higher Channel

I found a name and number in one of the newsletters from someone local who was offering an introduction to conscious channeling of our own spiritual essence. I called the number and set up an appointment. A nice woman introduced herself and welcomed me into her home. I sat down, and she asked me some basic questions about my experience with meditation or connecting within. I hadn't really tried either. I was just a newbie to any actual practice, but I had a lot of information!

She explained that she would project certain emotions, and I was to try and guess the emotion. She asked me to close my eyes and clear my mind. I did both. She began to project an emotion and asked me what I felt. I told her it felt like peace. Then I felt love. There were a couple more, and she ended on anger, which was the easiest to detect. This was without sight or sound and quite fascinating. She talked about energy and how everything we do has an energetic component and that we are all made of energy. Emotions are energy in motion. It was a good session, and it was nice to meet someone with similar interests.

Back to the San Francisco channeling session.

Montaviel noticed Brent seemed conflicted and said, "It's okay. You can talk about it." Brent, getting emotional, replied, "All right. Um, can we talk about Alisal and what part he plays in my life?"

"He plays no more, no less than what Somé plays," Montaviel answered. "He plays no more or no less than what your mother plays. No more, no less than what anyone else plays. He is a player in your role, part of your experience. Players come and go. The experiences come and go."

"It's hard for me to accept that they go so fast," Brent admitted.

Montaviel responded, "I remember your mother saying the same thing when it was time for you to leave. She felt the same way. Why did it have to go so fast and end so abruptly? Why can't we take time? And yet, you didn't look back at her and feel what you're feeling now about an experience ending. It's not any different."

"Parents are supposed to let their children go. I want somebody to share my life with," Brent said.

"Why do you think it can't happen again? Why do you think it won't happen?" Montaviel asked.

"I don't know. I'm losing hope. I mean, I want it to happen, but…I don't know," Brent replied.

"You want it to happen with one person," Montaviel pointed out.

"I do," Brent admitted.

"Do you think of yourself as less of a person with someone else?" Montaviel asked.

"The problem is, I see myself as stronger with Alisal than without him. I don't feel whole when he's not there. Maybe it's because I don't understand who I am. It goes back to a conversation I had with a professor in college who wouldn't let me audition for a role because he said I didn't know who I was. He said I didn't know how to be me, but I don't know who 'me' is," Brent confessed.

"Exactly, most of us don't," Montaviel agreed.

"I felt closest to myself, at least I thought I did, with Alisal around," Brent said, sobbing.

"All I can say is love has no face," Montaviel said.

"Okay," Brent replied.

Montaviel continued, "If you go through life only doing what you think is right for you, then stop everything you are doing because life as you know it has ended. There's no more experience to have because you won't allow it. In the last eight years, there have been 167 times when you had the chance to experience something new, but because of your determination and choice not to feel or accept a new experience, you looked the other way."

Montaviel explained, "Is that bad? No. Is that good? No. It's just the way it is. But it will never stop. The experience is ongoing. The chances in that experience are endless. And in all those other people, you could have had just as much, if not more, than what you had with Alisal. The feeling, the love, the compassion—every sense you want to feel could have been felt if you hadn't looked the other way. There is enough time in your life to experience people who can give you more than you ever imagined. They're there. Just stop closing your eyes. Keep your eyes and mind open."

Brent asked, "With Michael Jervane, was that a good experience? Did I turn my back on it?"

"No," Montaviel replied, "but you did have a little push into that one," he added with a laugh. "But those are the things I'm talking about. You can push yourself and experience all that needs to be, because in all those experiences, you'll find many people who you can share everything with, who you can give everything you feel is worth giving.

"But don't diminish yourself in doing it," Montaviel continued. "Don't give yourself away. You've never had an experience like that. It's foreign to you. But there are people in your life who can offer you that experience where you don't have to give yourself away and can remain yourself, still growing and feeling what you want to feel.

"It's always there. Just don't close yourself off to it. It knocks on the door all the time."

Brent sighed and said, "Can you give me an idea of who I am? All I see is, you know..."

"It's not what you see; it's what you feel," Montaviel replied. "So, when you interpret what you feel as what you see, it's not the same. What you feel is what you feel. If you want to interpret that feeling and create something about yourself so you can see it, you want emotion to have a face."

"Is what I feel, me?" Brent asked.

"What you feel is what you feel. It's not you. Don't identify yourself with what you feel. There are many parts of you to explore and many parts to get in touch with. You have no idea what's inside. But what we see inside and work with is like another world. Don't close that world off. You are more than what you think you are, as long as you don't let what you think be dictated by what you feel."

Brent asked, "Is there any guidance you can give me for the future, besides not closing off these experiences?"

"No. What you need to know, you already know. Right now, you know more than your current reality lets you realize. But you know it. The reality you deal with daily doesn't allow you to experience who you really are. But who you are is there, and you are in touch with it. It's just that your current reality doesn't let you experience it. You get slight glimpses, fleeting thoughts."

"Am I okay living where I am?" Brent asked.

Montaviel nodded. "And you would be no less perfect living somewhere else. There's nothing you can lose. Where you feel comfortable and can grow best is where you're at. If you need to move on, you will. I don't see anything stopping you. Never has."

Brent said, "I can't think of anything else."

Alavan then asked, "You were talking about going through the experiences everyone goes through. Why do we do that? Is it just the unfoldment of life? Is that what it's all about?"

Montaviel replied, "We want to put so much more into what is actually there. There's nothing complex about living an experience. Do you find complexities in breathing? Do you find complexities in looking out of your eyes? Then why place complexity in the experience?"

Alavan reflected, "When I look back at where I am now, I know I couldn't have gotten here without Spirit. I couldn't imagine doing it by myself. If I hadn't really listened, I wouldn't be here today."

Montaviel smiled, "You could not have done it any other way."

"Your experiences will move much more rapidly when you don't place limits on them. Things would move rapidly if you didn't place so many limits on every experience. You place hundreds of thousands of limits on every experience—hundreds of thousands. There shouldn't be any. That doesn't lessen or heighten the experience. It doesn't change the feeling you have for someone else."

Brent, emotionally, said, "Every day and every night since he left, I have so much hope in my heart for him to come back. But I know I'm putting a face on it."

Montaviel replied, "What you ask is a beautiful, honest expression. Yet, we are limited in how we can help when you don't truly believe in it. The feeling and sincerity aren't there. We want to believe you, but there's nothing in your reality that tells you that it's worth believing in. Your emotion rules your thoughts. So, when another part of you rules your thoughts, the sincerity of the suggestion is acknowledged, but we can do nothing because you don't allow us. When you let us be part of your expression, we won't let you down. We're there. But we have to work within your reality and what you believe is real for you. We have to let that take precedence over your experience." Montaviel looked at a burning cigarette and picked it up by the burning end, seemingly without intending to smoke it but trying to accommodate a request from Somé to do so.

Brent asked, "By allowing you, is that removing the limits I've set?"

Montaviel nodded. "How does that make you feel?" Brent slowly shook his head. "I know how it makes you feel. Why do I want to hear from you? Because I want you to understand what it means. One part of you constantly fights with the other, and the fight never stops."

Brent sobbed, "I know. Because I don't want to let go."

Montaviel gently replied, "You don't want the fight to stop. When you truly believe that peace of mind, soul, body, and emotion is real, it'll be there. We can only give you what is real for you. We can't give you more or less than what is real for you."

Brent, shaking his head slowly, said, "I don't know how to do it."

Montaviel smiled and nodded, "Yes, you do. Oh, yes, you do."

Brent emotionally asked, "Is it okay that I continue to see Alisal?"

"Of course. Why wouldn't it be?" Montaviel replied.

Brent continued, "Well, it just seems so difficult, you know?" Montaviel flipped the cigarette around and tried to draw smoke from it unsuccessfully. He turned it over to see if it was working correctly.

Brent started laughing at the cigarette fiasco, "You didn't smoke in form, did you?" He laughed even more.

Montaviel, smiling, said, "Strange little thing, isn't it?" He continued to turn it over a few times. "Where does it all go?"

Brent, still laughing, said, "It's one of those little things we enjoy here." Montaviel finally drew smoke from the cigarette. "I'm sorry I got upset with you last night and the universe. It just gets so frustrating at times. I feel like no one seems to listen to me."

Montaviel reassured him, "We listen more than you can imagine. Listening is what we're best at. We don't get much practice in doing, but listening, oh yeah. We listen until we don't want to listen anymore." There was smiling and laughter all around.

Brent said, "You get tired of listening to me, I'm sure."

Alavan added, "You and everybody else. We all do the same."

Montaviel said, "It's part of the whole experience." He took another drag of the cigarette, lowered it, then looked to his right as if listening to Somé, then to his left, blew out, and checked for smoke, causing more laughter.

Montaviel observed, "So, at least the fear is diminished."

Brent nodded in agreement, "I did have a lot of fear coming into this. I wasn't sure. And Somé told me that it was pretty much everything I've heard already."

Montaviel said, "We can chalk this up as one more unrealistic expectation on your part."

Brent agreed, "It's true. It's true."

Montaviel continued, "It's something that you're a MASTER at. It's good to be a master at something." He smiled and nodded.

Brent chuckled, "Okay. Rub it in." Everyone laughed.

Montaviel said, "It enriches. It does enrich the experience. But you've reached the limit of your enrichment. It can't enrich anymore. There's too much information that you already know. So, from now on, it diminishes. It takes away from the wholeness of you. That's not our choice, and it's not your conscious choice. But it does. It diminishes you. You've seen it

A Higher Channel

happen over and over. Don't let what you know overrun your emotion or let your emotion be controlled by the information you have."

Chapter 3: Meeting The Walk-Ins

One of the newsletters had an invitation to meet Savizar and Silarra, the walk-ins, in the Santa Cruz mountains during a half-day event in October 1989. Somé and I decided to go since it was less than an hour away, just up Highway 1.

We drove into the Santa Cruz mountains and up a winding road to the house hosting the walk-ins. When we arrived, we rang the doorbell and were welcomed in. They were already talking, so we quietly took our seats on the floor.

They spoke about their mission to co-create Heaven on Earth with many planetary masters who had not yet awakened their part of the grand drama unfolding on Planet Earth today. They explained that they were the third team of walk-ins who had inhabited their bodies. The first two teams, from 1986-1988, came to prepare beings for the planetary shift. As each team of walk-ins enters form, "it signals the arrival of a higher octave of divine force and the emergence of new, more refined, and loving technologies to support the co-creation of Heaven on Earth" (Savizar and Silarra 1989, 171).

They discussed the systems we all buy into: credit, jobs, families, and the agreements that guide our decisions every day and for the rest of our lives. These agreements leave little room for following our own spirit to co-create Heaven on Earth. We become slaves to these agreements, with rules of behavior that limit our expression. We edit ourselves because we want to be right and control everything. We are masters of limitation.

They shared that everyone is perfect just the way they are and that being judgmental can be a method of discernment to figure out who deserves your time and energy. Following your spirit is about doing what comes to you without filtering. It also means not caring if anyone hears you or reacts in a certain way. If we think about those things, we start to edit what we say or don't say anything at all.

It was a great session. At one point, we sat in a circle in silence, just looking at each other. It was uncomfortable but a great exercise to notice our triggers to "fix" the situation.

I loved the honesty, fierceness, and purity of their messages.

A couple of months later, I started dating a girl, Paige, whom I met at the local theater. We saw that there was a walk-in seminar in Sedona, Arizona, in January or February. Somé wanted to go but couldn't take that much time off, so Paige and I went. We first sent a deposit and pictures of ourselves. I remember the freeways covered in snow, as was Sedona. It was quiet and beautiful when we arrived. The walk-ins were Savizar (male) and Silarra (female), though they never mentioned gender.

Although they were walk-ins and brought tremendous wisdom, they also channeled higher spirits. Savizar channeled Alarius, and Silara channeled Polaria. We spent four days and three nights with them in their large home in Sedona. There were about 12 attendees from all walks of life. I remember one guy was a jeweler who brought stones to sell, and another person made cool clothes with interdimensional symbols and stars—very flowy and comfortable.

I vividly remember walking in the front door for the first time, perhaps a little over-excited, and shouting a big, "Hey!" I was quickly redirected and asked to place our things in the room downstairs on the left and come back to join the conversation. It was the kind of correction an overzealous puppy might get from its mother. I knew they meant business. I found them to be very welcoming and friendly, but also very direct.

We sat in the living room with Savizar and Silarra at one end and formed a sort of rectangle around the room. The messages were very similar to what we heard in Santa Cruz. They used toning with their voices to break energetic patterns in the room, much like music or singing bowls, but with more intensity. One of their main sayings is, "The universe rearranges itself to accommodate your picture of reality." This was difficult for me to understand for years. It's like the idea of manifestation that you hear about today but with a twist. What you experience daily is as much about what you believe and imply about life rather than what you want from life. For change to happen, we have to start living differently, little by little. It's like the quote, "Fake it until you make it."

Another saying of theirs is, "Follow your spirit without hesitation." I've always asked how we can tell the difference between our spirit and our own conscious thoughts. They would say to follow what you believe to be spirit until you feel different and gain some discernment about what was spirit and what wasn't. Then you keep doing that until you gain more discernment, and so on. I've also found that when my internal response is fear and doubt, it's clearly not Spirit. We all have this internal dialogue that responds with fear, warning, or some reason not to do something.

I recall on the second day in Sedona, the subject of planetary shift and expansion came up. Savizar spoke of more light beings coming for the expansion. I said, "Is this like the dolphins beaching themselves?" He said that, yes, it is, and that we had a couple of dolphin spirits here with us today (he motioned toward Paige and me). I would later learn that I had a few lives as a dolphin and that this was only my second life in human form. Most people average around 25 – 40 lives in human form. Validation of that and many other bits of information would come through Somé over the years.

The Sedona event was full of discussions about realities, how we trap ourselves, and the evolution that will take place if we recognize the limitations that we and others place in front of us while continuing to follow our spirits without hesitation. Savizar, Silarra, and the original walk-ins created Extraterrestrial Earth Mission to share many of these sessions in books and other formats. I remember listening to some of their sessions on cassette tapes in my old 1979 Honda Accord hatchback!

Back to the San Francisco session.

Montaviel said, "You're no more privileged knowing what you know today than anybody else. Everyone else finds out in different ways."

He continued, "This is our way of staying in touch and communicating. But don't think you're any more privileged to do what you're doing now than anyone else. There are many other ways this can happen."

Brent mentioned, "Somé and I heard a song today. Can you give us some insights as to why that song was so important today?"

"We were all listening," Montaviel said with a smile. "Because it brings a new reality. Anytime something new comes into your life that changes your way of thinking, it's a miracle. It gives you a new way to think about yourself, other people, your experiences, and your dreams. It was very appropriate for you," Montaviel added. "It wasn't a mistake."

Brent agreed, "I do like the words, 'seeing a bit of you in everything'."

"Very important," Montaviel emphasized. "Things don't just happen. Don't think that it was your choice or control that made these things happen. We like to take a little credit for a few things." There was laughter.

Alavan asked, "How can you guys do that? I mean, you're in spirit and a little thing like a song or a word on TV from another company—there are so many details on the planet. How can you keep track of them all? Is it just energy that you move into our minds and eyes to see these words?"

Montaviel, smiling, explained, "The movement of energy is broken up into three parts: what we experience within, what we see, and what we hear. It's easy for us to take those three and in a third-dimensional reality, place all three into one. I can let you experience something new by letting you hear one word. I can trigger a response in a million people at once with one word. The energy for that is there."

"So, do you know exactly what form it will take on the planet, like whether you'll hear something on the radio or see it on TV or get a CD in the mail? Do you know specifically what it will be?" Alavan asked.

"We know specifically," Montaviel confirmed.

"You guys know a lot," Alavan commented.

"It's our job," Montaviel said with a smile, and everyone laughed.

"It just seems so big to be able to do that," Alavan remarked.

"You see limits," Montaviel replied. "The master of limits here (he nodded toward Brent) can explain how to limit all these little things into one small group. When you limit everything, you make it so simple for us. So simple.

"Look at a ray of sunshine coming through the window. It doesn't take much. That's all we need to do. We do this many times a day, looking for things to trigger a response, letting you know there's something more real about you than what you know within the experience. Sometimes we have to make the response a little heavier. Since you have more information about yourselves now, the next response might be a slap across the face. The triggering becomes stronger; the responses become stronger. Our relentlessness in getting a point across is unending."

Montaviel explained, "Sometimes, our ruthlessness is heartbreaking. But things must be done when they need to be done, and we do not let up. You have to remember that you made the choice to let spirit become a conscious and evident experience in your life. You made that choice."

He continued, "After making that choice, it became overwhelming. That's why you had to limit the information and experience, because you were losing an unrealistic expectation in your experience that you felt wasn't good enough for you. So, we move faster and swifter, with a vengeance. We are relentless."

Montaviel added, "If you indicate that you wish for something else in your life, you'll have it tomorrow."

Alavan asked, "What do you mean?"

"He knows what I mean. In fact, I can arrange it within the next 30 seconds. I can have that phone ring in 30 seconds," Montaviel replied.

He continued, "The choice is still yours to make. I know Alavan finds choice perplexing." There was laughter.

Alavan said, "Well, it is kind of confusing."

Montaviel addressed Brent, "The choices you have are vast. This is how we set our direction and become who we want to be—by our own choices. You experience by your choice. But you think you're limited by your environment."

Montaviel clarified, "Yes, you are limited by the environment you chose to be in. Not because Spirit placed you there, but because you placed yourself there."

Alavan asked, "You mean, the third dimension?"

"Right. That is where your choice comes from. You still have a choice. The choice is yours," Montaviel answered.

Brent asked, "Was my relationship with Alisal meant to take this path, or did we make choices that ended it?"

"You ended it," Montaviel replied.

Brent was surprised. "I ended it?"

"By your choice to accept Spirit," Montaviel explained.

"To accept Spirit in my life?" Brent asked.

Montaviel nodded. "That, to me, is one of the most beautiful experiences anyone can have. That's when the heavens opened, and the realness of your life began."

Brent reflected on his experience with a prior reading by a psychic, "The first reading I had was correct, then. It said I would end the relationship. It would be my choice."

Alavan added, "It was very accurate because you guys also spoke to her (the other guide)?"

"It was very correct. We don't make mistakes," Montaviel said with a laugh.

"Somé puts tremendous amounts of faith and power into his actions. He can open the way for you in many ways. He can let you experience things you never dreamed possible if you allow it," Montaviel continued.

"And if he allows himself to do it," Montaviel added, readjusting his seating, smiling at Brent, and turning to look at Alavan.

Alavan said, "Thanks for coming."

Montaviel joked, "Are you shoving me out?" There was laughter.

Alavan replied, "No, I just wanted to say it."

Brent, getting emotional, said, "Spirit, I can't help but still have hope that..."

"What's wrong with having hope?" Montaviel asked.

Brent explained, "Well, I don't want to stop experiencing the things that happen to me. I'm suffering."

Montaviel clarified, "Realistic hope is believing that when I go to sleep tonight, I will wake up tomorrow. Unrealistic hope is believing I'll wake up tomorrow as a saint. But no more, no less the same hope. Hope has no face. Don't place a face on hope. Hope is a feeling, an experience, a reality. It's a precious thing to have. But stop only wanting one experience with one face. Life is about experiencing everyone and everything equally. No one gets any less than anyone else. When you start doing that, you lose. You lose big time."

Montaviel continued, "I know the direction you want. I really do. I know it seems useless, but it's not. And it's not unrealistic to think that you're experiencing what you're going through. It's not unrealistic. It's very real. It's very real to me. It's very real to you. But we have to play a game and the game we're going to play is 'Love Has No Face.' Experience has no face. My emotions have no face. Anyone can bring up the same emotion by smelling a flower or falling in love. One has no greater power than the other unless you give it that power and you only give it that power because you're working on a reality based on something unrealistic to begin with. It's just not real. You're asking for guidance. We're giving you guidance. And in giving you the guidance you don't want to accept the guidance. You say, 'No, the guidance you're giving me is too painful. The guidance you're giving to me is unrealistic' No, this is real."

Brent acknowledged, "I know it's real."

"But it's uncomfortable," Montaviel pointed out.

"Very," Brent agreed.

"Look at the learning process. Look at the richness of what you have. God, it's unreal. There are so many people who would do anything to have what you had. I can bring them here by the hundreds, and they would say, 'Let me have at least one moment of what you had. Just give me one moment,'" Montaviel said.

He continued, "That's the turmoil many people live under. They live under different guises, saying 'Just give me one moment.' And I can say the same to you. Give yourself one real moment, and I will give you a life you can't even fathom. That's realistic hope. It's the dream of today and the hope of tomorrow. It's real. It's inside and waiting to come out, and I'm ready to bring it out. I'm ready when you are. Just let me know when. Then I need to do a little work and just listen." Montaviel smiled, and Brent laughed.

Montaviel added, "I don't want to diminish what you feel."

Brent, sobbing, said, "I know you don't."

"But I know exactly what you feel," Montaviel answered.

Brent said, "See, I want to share this with Alisal because he is part of my life. But I don't know what to say without sounding like I'm preaching."

Montaviel replied, "He is part of your life. He was part of your life, and he still is." Brent nodded. "Alavan keeps quoting this little phrase to you that he thinks is quite appropriate, and I would probably have to agree. It came up about 1900 years ago: 'casting your pearls before swine.' He just seems to think that holds so much impact and glory and there's so much intelligence in it." Everyone laughed.

Montaviel continued, "And it does. It has more meaning than people realize. So, when you have something to say, say it to someone who cares and understands. Say it where it counts. Give that emotion and feeling where it's due. Don't see the experience as less than it was. It was the most glorious, most beautiful experience you could've had."

"But don't think for a second that the next one isn't ready to come right behind it. And it is. It's just hard for you as people, in this contraption. This limited, very limited form of expression."

Chapter 4: An Unexpected Breakthrough

Paige and I returned to Monterey and moved in with an Austrian couple who made and distributed an alternative meat product to health food stores. They rented a house in Pebble Beach and needed roommates. It's a beautiful area, so we were in!

One night, we had Somé over and shared details about the trip to Sedona, describing toning and how it worked. We decided to give a demonstration and suggested that he visualize a tunnel with light at the end. We started quietly with low tones and then slowly moved up to higher tones, varying the intensity and volume. After a few minutes, I noticed Somé was starting to fall asleep. His head lowered, and his eyes closed. We toned a bit more and then woke him up. He said he visualized the tunnel and that's all he remembered until we woke him.

Somé felt he was at a crossroads after leaving his old life. One day, he told me to meet him after work at Seal Rock Creek Beach on 17-Mile Drive. He looked tired, but I knew if I was there after work, he would be too. When I arrived, I saw his car parked nearby and spotted him sitting on a tall rock at the ocean's edge. I called him in and asked what he was doing there. He said he prayed for the ocean to take him because he felt he had no purpose in life. He was very emotional, saying his life was crashing down. With tears running down his face, he said that he had left everything and had nobody. He was very lonely and felt that way his whole life, he shared. He had just left his wife, and the place he was living had a gas leak and explosion a couple of days earlier, forcing everyone to move out. I hugged him and told him he had new friends now and that we would take care of him. He then moved into the house Paige and I lived in, along with the Austrian couple.

I have read from many authors, including Savizar and Silarra, that we live on the third dimension. Worldly energies without form (ghosts and other spirits) reside in the fourth dimension, and what we understand as heaven is the fifth dimension. There are higher dimensions, but they are iterations of the fifth. Most people have higher spirits on the fifth, seventh, tenth, and fourteenth dimensions. It's not about one being better than the other. The idea of better/worse and good/bad is a third-dimensional reality. It's hard to imagine a life outside of opposites because we've lived in this reality for so long. As children, we learn to label and group everything, giving it all an identity that is fixed. This rigidity shapes our thoughts. Even though nature seems effortless and random, laws control its every ebb and flow. This is true for solar systems, universes, planets, and people. That's why we are fascinated with things outside this boxed reality. We love fantasy, miraculous stories, and dreams. It's the pull of our spirit and the supernatural speaking to us, begging us to be free.

I've always loved the supernatural, but not Somé. This was all very weird and scary for him. He didn't understand much of what Savizar and

A Higher Channel

Silarra said at the Santa Cruz event, and he certainly didn't know what to make of what was happening to him.

After Somé's first channeling session, we had him over again a few nights later. This time, a new spirit came through. As we began toning, his head nodded slowly, and when it came back up, the spirit said with utter fear, "Somé gonna get Bacha! Somé gonna get Bacha!" It screamed urgency and unpredictability, so we began toning loudly and asked Spirit for help. His head lowered again and then came back up, this time with a huge smile—bigger than I'd ever seen. He was giggling uncontrollably. This was clearly a different spirit and very friendly. He kept smiling and giggling, mostly with his eyes closed. Then he said, "Have to be serious" and tried to force a straight face, but it didn't work. Back to smiling and giggling. "Must be serious," he said more forcefully, as if receiving a command. But the smile crept back. It was entertaining. I tried to engage him. "What is your name?" I asked. "Somé," he said between giggles. "Why are you here?" I asked—more giggling. "I'm supposed to be serious," he said, "but I want to play. I want to have fun!" He seemed to be talking to someone. Then the smile was gone for a second as if he was reprimanded, but it quickly returned. Then he was gone. This playful spirit was no threat. We later learned it was one of Somé's fifth-dimensional spirits. He chose to adopt this spirit's name, as it was the first of his own that he channeled. It would not be the last time we saw this little guy.

Somé shared that he was having strange thoughts in his head about bizarre things. These thoughts didn't come from him, so he knew they came from somewhere else. He had thoughts about dimensions, stars, planetary expansion, and a higher sense of who he is. He felt a newfound awareness and the ability to do things with energy and feeling. He had never thought about this stuff before. In fact, he was always put down as a child, and much of that carried into his adulthood. It was all very confusing for him. After hearing something, he would usually come to me and ask if I'd heard of it before, and I usually had a reference for it. Most of all, I reassured him that he wasn't going crazy.

Return to the San Francisco session

Montaviel said, "Everything is extremely limited. When you get a bit of information and understanding of what your conscious and subconscious mind can do, you'll really see those limits."

Alavan asked, "Is that why you guys keep reminding us all the time? Because we fall so easily into one mood or emotion and stay there?"

Montaviel replied, "You're like a small child with an attention span of about two seconds. Adults are the same. I can focus on a small child, uncorrupted by thoughts and experiences, and let that child hold on to the past experience of the lifetime before him and enhance what we have. We have about six million children in the world we work with daily. That's a tiny fraction compared to your capabilities."

A Higher Channel

He continued, " Six million children in the world that we have an ongoing moment-to-moment expression with, that we can let them experience everything that's being unfolded from their past into the moment of now to create the future – all in one existence. Because they aren't blocked by authoritative figures. We have been given these children. We've been given these children from the day that they're born. Their parents say, 'This is my gift to God. This is my gift to Spirit. Do what needs to be done,' and we do. It's the most beautiful experience because they aren't bombarded or filtered. The real truth that lies within all of us is exposed."

Alavan asked, "What would these children look like to us?"

Montaviel answered, "You'd know them by listening to them talk."

Alavan clarified, "Because it's different?"

"Yes. But they also have human friends. They're everyday people you'd see on the street," Montaviel explained.

Alavan asked, "You mean they also have imaginary friends?"

"No, it's just that their minds and environment don't warp their sense of self. They aren't diminished in any way," Montaviel said. "But when you think of only six million children experiencing their wholeness daily, it's beautiful but also sad. We could have six billion instead of six million."

He added, " That's where the choice is. The choice that God has let you have in these life forms. It's part of an ongoing process. And it's a beautiful process."

Alavan asked, "Is it all about having that unique experience?"

Montaviel replied, "Do you think me coming here has happened many times before with this group, this conversation? No. The communication has been ongoing, but this specific experience is new. But in a third-dimensional sense, I look around and think, 'What for?' Because what I see has no bearing on what I know to be real."

He continued, "Your living—this is what you call living—is limited. You close yourself off in a little box. This is a reality based on the generational process of experience, but this (pointing to his heart) is the experience. You don't need this (pointing to the walls) to have an experience. Each person includes about three million things in their life and calls it experience. It doesn't add or take away from it, but it still has nothing to do with it. As time passes on the planet, it takes longer and longer for people to find their true experience because there's more and more stuff."

Alavan asked, "And it's faster and faster? And is everybody speeding up?"

Montaviel said, "You lose this (pointing to his heart). They don't use this (pointing to his head). They don't know what the true experience is."

He asked, "Do you think who you were before you came into this life thousands of years ago was any less than the experience you're having now? And yet you surround yourself with millions of things that you count as your experience. Are you enhanced by that? Do you get more out of it? You could experience the same feelings and emotions 6,000 years ago, not limited by a little square box, and it would be faster and cleaner with no interruption."

Alavan asked, "Really?"

Montaviel replied, "So what people experienced then is much different than what you experience now."

Alavan added, "It takes longer?"

Montaviel nodded, "Much longer. Because you limit yourself."

Alavan mentioned, "The spirit Alarius talked about how technology makes it easier for people to move from one reality to the next, and times are accelerated. So, is that different?"

Montaviel explained, "To put it in terms you can understand, 6,000 years ago, a form moved through experiences much faster because they weren't bogged down by things. The experience was truer and cleaner. Today, people need a different stimulation than 6,000 years ago. The stimulation has to be fast, quick, and effective."

Montaviel said, "So, you asked about technology giving people more experiences at a faster pace. Yes, it happens and has to because of the limited time left. So, it's not that technology is better than before; it's just necessary to speed things up because of the limits you've placed on yourselves. By whose choice? Your choice."

He continued, "So, when you think you can fool us with these gadgets, we turn them around and use them for our benefit. But it's actually more power to you."

Montaviel added, "So, you see there's a purpose and reason behind everything, even though I look and ask, 'Why?' because it doesn't add anything new to my experience. Gadgets are supposed to do something, but I have no reference for them. Like these burnable things," he said, nodding at the cigarettes.

Alavan asked, "Do you want another one, or does Somé?"

Montaviel laughed and replied, "Oh, him?" He nodded to the side.

Alavan said, "You figure his form will live, right?"

Montaviel replied, "I'm sure. At least past this experience." There was laughter. "So, having a gadget is just a formality."

Alavan said, "This may be the last time you see one of these." There was more laughter.

Montaviel said, "I don't think so. Well, I know it won't be the last time. But it's nice to have informality instead of the stringent fear placed on so many things. It makes it easier to comprehend and more believable for you," looking at Brent. "Of course, we could bring Bion (a higher-dimensional spirit of Brent's, from the 14th dimension) through and really start a party." They all laughed.

Alavan asked, "And he would last about what, 10 seconds?"

"Yes," Montaviel smiled.

Brent asked, "Can you tell me a little about Bion (14th dimension) and Kaes (7th dimension)? I really don't know much about them."

Montaviel explained, "Bion is the highest part of your captive reality. He is the highest expression and thinking in your reality. The 14th dimension is beyond your comprehension. It prepares your spirit for transformation. He is like a leader in you, but there's no connection because there are many things outside your realm of reality that have no bearing on the limited expression that you're in. And you're in a very limited expression. So, stop placing your feelings on something so limited to begin with."

He continued, "Because once you use the expansiveness of mind and you open your mind to the experience, whoa, hold on."

Alavan said, "So, it seems like as we grow, we limit our current self to build a new self. How do we ever progress?"

Montaviel replied, "Your interpretation is correct in your reality. Everything is in a reverse cycle. Somé talks about reversal energies. Spirit calls it a reverse cycle, and we're in it."

Alavan asked, "With who?"

Montaviel replied, "The universe. The universe is in a reverse cycle."

"Why not just call it a cycle?" Alavan questioned.

"Because it's a reverse cycle," Montaviel said. "As the new wave started."

"Do you mean our system?" Alavan asked.

Montaviel explained, "Right now, we are in a reverse cycle. We are reversing to an expansion. Why call it reversal? Because if we were expanding and moving at the same pace as the energy, your heads would blow up. So, we are in a slowdown mode. Only in your reality do you see things moving faster and faster. But in our reality, we have to slow this down to match universal energy. So, it creates a reverse cycle. It may not make sense, but that's the best way I can explain it."

Alavan asked, "So, there are no forms on planets when we're in this expansive mode? You're saying our heads would blow up because it's expanding?"

"If you're talking about stars or other energies on different planes, of course," Montaviel replied.

"Yeah, but not dense, third-dimensional forms?" Alavan asked.

Montaviel shook his head. "Why can't your spaceships detect life somewhere else?" There was laughter.

Alavan said, "Because they're dense, right?"

"Have you ever seen a camera take pictures of spirit?" Montaviel asked.

"They try," Alavan answered.

"We can't take a picture of your emotion," Montaviel said.

Alavan mentioned, "We were watching a movie recently where someone asked another person to 'bring out your emotion and show it to me.'"

"Getting back to your emotion, feeling, or thought, thought is the strongest energy on the planet. Show me a picture of the wind and tell me there's no existence for it. We know there is because we feel it. How can we feel something we can't see? And yet people want to tell you that we are not real," Montaviel explained.

Alavan asked, "What is with those people?"

"No more, no less than what you believe. What they believe to be true, they believe to be true," Montaviel replied. "Skeptics are necessary for the evolution of life."

A Higher Channel

He continued, "This is where we have the reversal energy. This is how we keep the cycle moving at a slower pace. It's essential to have."

Chapter 5: Zitron

After a couple of months of continuous information from Spirit, Somé told me he thought, "Ok, if all this information is here, it must be for a reason, and I need to know more about what's going on." Then he said the information was non-stop, and he couldn't stop it from coming. So, he figured he needed to try and give a voice to all the information.

He said about the next time he channeled, "I just kept saying the name Somé over and over until finally, I felt like I was getting a clear connection. It was a very strange feeling, almost like not being yourself. It's like being in a dream but awake. I remember talking to you a lot about that, and that's when I wanted to bring Somé back. We were discussing the higher spirits, how many we have, who they are, and that's when Zitron came in and took over. I didn't deliberately channel Zitron. I was trying to connect with Somé again, but Zitron came in. That was the first time I heard a distinct voice, not a thought. It sounded like my own but was clearly not me because I wasn't talking or thinking. And that's when it all started."

Zitron arrived with a warm smile and a gentle voice, saying, "Hello. We are here to bring about wonderful things. This is only the beginning of a process of expansion of light happening across this planet, as it has on many planets before this one." He mentioned we were going to have people over at the house. And then, just like that, he was gone.

A Higher Channel

A week or so later, we had about ten or twelve people over to the house, mostly from work, for a channeling session. We were all sitting in the living room in a sort of circle with candles, dim lights, and meditative music playing. Somé began, and a couple of minutes later, we heard a big boom outside that shook the house. As the lights blinked on and off, we sat startled and began looking at each other and around to see what might be going on. Just then, Somé's head lifted, his chest expanded, and we heard a "pop" from his chest area. Another of his higher spirits, Botra, exclaimed, "We are here to do great things!" I asked, "What was all that noise and shaking?" He said, "I like to make an entrance!" We all chuckled. He said that accelerated times were ahead of us. Somé would begin important work toward the expansion of light for people and the planet. He also mentioned that he was someone of very few words. As he left, the candles flickered, and he was gone.

Several nights later, we were standing outside just after midnight, and the fog was thick, as it often is in the Bay Area. Zitron came through and, after taking a deep breath in and exhaling, said, "Can you feel the life in the air? How wonderful it must be to be able to smell... to embrace this... all of this is beauty." Referring to the fog, he continued, "Do you see the angels in disguise? Can you feel them in the air? Somé asked for protection, and there are four angels provided as a protective shield. They will be with you for the rest of your lives." We began to walk down the street and continued onto a pathway at the edge of a nearby golf course. It was peaceful, with the fog providing a layer of dew and insulating against any ambient noise. We approached a stream where hundreds of frogs were croaking. It added to the serene feeling. Suddenly, the frogs stopped, but we weren't close enough to startle them. I looked over at Zitron, who stopped dead in his tracks, looked skyward, raised his hand, closed his eyes, and said some words in a different language, "Et teta to mo pa," which translates to "We have to stop." He left, and Botra came in, quickly surveying the sky through his hand and saying, "I need help now." He quickly left, and another spirit came in, exclaiming, "Go back!" with both arms raised. Then he lowered his arms and head, and Somé was back. The frogs started croaking again. I asked Somé what happened. He said there was an energy approaching from another star system that wanted to stop everything Somé was doing. The energy was large and strong enough to require Source (God) to send them back. It was both a very scary and powerful experience for me.

The next walk-in event was less than a month later in San Rafael, California, just across the San Francisco Bay, north of San Francisco. What led to that event would be another soul-shaking experience.

Back to the San Francisco session

Alavan asked, "How can someone live with a fifth-dimensional reality without being aware of that dimension?"

Montaviel replied, "That's the majority of those who have passed through the fifth dimension. They had no idea. You don't need the terminology or even to know what the words mean. You just need to follow what's being said, follow your thoughts, and experience the feeling behind it."

Alavan asked, "The biggest question everybody asks is how do you know the difference?"

Montaviel responded, "How do you not know the difference? You tell me."

Alavan continued, "People say, 'I don't know if it's my emotion driving my action or what to listen to.' It can be hard to tell if it's an old thought or a new thought."

Montaviel said, "The experience tells you. You've been through the experience enough to know what you're following, and it sure isn't your thought."

Alavan noted, "But in hindsight, it's easy to check that, you know?"

Montaviel replied, "What do you think experience is for? Experience is the only tool we have to teach a limited expression. When you're dealing with a limited expression, experience is the only teacher."

He continued, "But when you let the experience become the reality so that you experience no more, life is over. You can't get enough space or time."

Montaviel added for Brent, "Meeting Somé at the time you did was no coincidence. Remember what you were thinking several weeks before that happened? The answers you were looking for after an upsetting experience. People like him come into your life to make a bigger impact than the experience you just finished. One moment with one person can be more powerful than a million years with another. One moment. That moment is no less than a million years that you can give to someone else. I would have to say it's more powerful because if you can gain an experience in one moment, think of the power behind what that moment held."

Montaviel said, "When something else lasts a million years, you think if it lasts longer, it has to be better. No. If it lasts longer, it's probably because you're confused."

Brent asked, "But what about people who meet and stay together for the rest of their lives? Is there no meaning to that?"

Montaviel replied, "There's a lot of meaning to that because that's where you place your reality. But just because someone is together for 25 years doesn't mean that experience is better than one that lasted one moment. Longevity is not the healer of all feelings; the healer of all feelings comes in one moment, not in a lifetime."

He continued, "You're giving up one moment to hold on to an unrealistic expectation that you think will give you a lifetime of moments. It's not what you asked us for. If you're not willing and able to accept what you ask for, it can be changed very fast. We're good at this."

Montaviel explained, "People often think that when someone comes back, it's nice. But in whose reality is this nice? The reality of thinking that longevity is the answer to happiness. No. When someone comes back, it's often because it's the easiest road to take. It's too hard to face a new reality every day and that's what you asked for. You asked for no less than to have a new existence within yourself. And we take that to be a ready sign because of experiences that went on within you in the past five years. And this gives us the opportunity to say, okay, he's asking, let's show him what this really means. We understand totally. We understand more than you will understand what it means."

Brent said, "I don't want to keep going through this. I don't want to meet someone one day, then meet someone two days later, and then someone else two days later. That doesn't seem meaningful to me."

Montaviel replied, "That doesn't seem meaningful to me either, and that's not what I'm saying. You're giving someone else's relationship longevity as credibility for being good. In this day and age, longevity doesn't mean good."

Brent admitted, "Longevity to me seems safer."

Montaviel said, "Longevity in your expectations of your reality is good. But don't look at everybody else's and say it's good."

Brent explained, "I'm not saying it's always good, but a long-term relationship, especially a monogamous one, seems healthier. Going through joys and hardships together seems better to me. Longevity sounds like a good thing."

Montaviel agreed, "I understand. I couldn't agree with you more. But I think you're confused about what you're asking for. We're trying to give you exactly what you asked for. We want you to have that long-term relationship. But we want you to be you in the process. And we can't give you both. We can't give you a fantasy. We can't give you your true expression of who your reality says you are and put a different face on it. We can't do that. We won't do that. That would be to me, in your reality sense, the cruelest thing that I can do – to put you through the next 40 years of hell. Pure hell of never knowing who you really are, never feeling your whole existence. Oh, we could put that face there. We could put that face there tomorrow morning, and we could make sure that face stays there."

Montaviel continued, "But you are no longer you. Gone. No need for us. You're in control. And believe me, there are a lot of people out there that are doing that perfectly fine. Perfectly wonderful. We accept that. We are good listeners," Montaviel said with a smile, bringing chuckles all around.

"That's not what you asked for." Montaviel focused his gaze on Brent. "And we won't give up until you say it's time to give up. All it takes is one true thought, and that face can stay forever. But don't expect happiness or wholeness. The hope inside you, the love, is there. You know it, but you don't want to listen to it. The feeling of love is huge. I know you don't want to give that up for just a face. Love and emotion have no face. Don't place one there. Not now. Not now."

He added, "It stops you from experiencing something else. But don't confuse yourself by thinking that the short-term relationship that you had was bad because it was short. It wasn't. It was to show you the richness of yourself. That's what that experience is for. What are some of the things that you've said within your own mind? 'I never thought that I was capable of feeling this.' Well, we proved you wrong. We said, oh, yes, you are capable. You are capable, but your misconception and your misguided way in the choice that you made was a visual choice. You let your emotion, and your eyes connect to one energy, and this is the only way that you see it."

Montaviel continued, "I see it as perfect. A perfect way to let you experience what you asked to feel. And then you say, 'Damn you for letting me do this.' Brent chuckled.

"But that's not what you asked for. There's always a risk and a chance. But there's no more risk in opening your heart to the universe than in crossing the street. It's actually riskier to cross the street. Yet, you limit your experience to little boxes, little driving devices, and little things. The experience is vast and endless. But don't ask for wholeness if you're not willing to feel it inside you." He then looks at Brent and tilts his head. "I know what you're thinking, and it's not true. It won't help and just confuses things."

He added, "It's not easy and isn't meant to be easy. If it were easy, where would the meaning be? Some people go through countless meaningless experiences. But what does that experience hold? Nothing. Because they'll have to do it 160 million times before they get a glimpse of what took you one moment, one moment for you. It may take 25 lifetimes for someone else, but you got that glimpse of yourself in one moment. My God, how much more richness do you want to be proven that what you have is real? It's all real. It's all there. I think that is just a tremendous, tremendous experience to feel within yourself and don't diminish it in any way! Don't diminish that within yourself."

Montaviel said, "It's glorious! That's what life is about. It's about having the feeling, and you have it. If you want a specific feeling with a specific face, it can happen. But we were also able to show you in your experience that you now hold as being real. So, it's a reality. You know how you felt, you know what you were going through, and you say, 'How can I have all the wondrous things of life in one hand and all the misery of myself in the other?' Because if we don't show you both at the same time, how will you be able to make a choice?"

He concluded, " You ask for one thing; we show it to you. Then we show you the reality of what that one thing holds. Now here's your choice. You hold on to the face that has the emotion and the love and lose who you are in the process. Or do we say, no, the face I had for that moment and that emotion showed me how beautiful and wonderful I really am? And we gave you your experience as soon as possible, to fulfill that same desire within yourself to know it's real. By God, it's real. And those experiences don't have to end. But your so-called loss of something, I can't comprehend that."

Brent said, shaking his head slowly, "I know. I know."

Montaviel replied, "I can't understand what you think you've lost. I can only see what you gain. Maybe you can explain what's lost? Is the person lost? I know where to find them."

Brent said, "I know where to find him, but... I've lost something tangible. I don't know how to explain it."

Montaviel responded, "Well, I know what you mean. I know more about what you mean than you know what you mean. The tangible part, the touch, the feel, the body, the look, everything combined in this one form you admired and loved. You asked for that, so we arranged it. If you had asked for something different, without a face, we could have provided that even quicker. Would that be any less an experience than the one you had? Oh, no, more. More of the experience. Because it would be energetically more of you, and there are more people in your past, 6,421 of them, who are just waiting to be a part of your life right now. Just in this town, there are 600 people, 20 of whom you know very well, connected to your past and not just fleeting connections. We're talking to mothers, fathers, aunts, uncles, brothers, sisters, cousins and more."

Alavan asked, "So, is it really that easy? People say, 'Oh, I'd really like this in my life,' but we tend to waffle often."

Montaviel reached for a cigarette, but it was backward. Alavan let him know, and he turned it around. Brent checked the camera and said it was fine. Montaviel flicked the lighter and felt the flame on his finger. He lit the cigarette and set it down on the placemat. Alavan moved it to the ashtray to avoid burning the placemat. Montaviel drank from the coffee cup and attempted to take a drag from the cigarette.

Alavan chuckled as he watched Montaviel and said, "It's like having Zitron here, just learning how to do things," he said, referring to a time when Zitron was present for a lunch outing and ate a pat of butter still inside the foil.

Montaviel joked, "Are you trying to take me to lunch? I'm not particular. But if it would enhance your reality of Spirit, I'll go to lunch with you."

Brent laughed and commented, "Being in the third dimension..."

"Sucks. In your terms," Montaviel replied.

Brent laughed and then asked, "Can you have a picture of the person you want to be with?"

Montaviel said, "As long as it's not unrealistic, sure. We don't have anything against that. Nothing at all."

A Higher Channel

Brent started to ask, "I mean, is that..."

Alavan clarified, "You mean form preferences?"

Brent said, "Form preferences, things like that?"

Montaviel replied, "I don't see anything wrong with it. That's the way you're made up."

Alavan added, "We're biologically predisposed."

Brent said, "We're attracted to things."

Montaviel explained, "There's a reason for that. It enhances part of your experience."

Alavan asked, "Would you say you can go overboard with that? Like, in this case, is it unrealistic?"

Montaviel explained, "Yeah, but you have to determine what's realistic and what isn't. It's hard, but your experience shows you. You've had two beautiful experiences: one unrealistic and one realistic. You figure out which is which."

Alavan asked, "And by realistic and unrealistic, you mean?"

Montaviel clarified, "In your terms, not mine. To enhance your reality. We gave you one very close after disposing of another. It was real."

Alavan asked, "So, is he confusing himself when he believes it's the other one that's more realistic?"

Montaviel said, "Yes. It's your choice. But we showed you it's possible."

Brent asked, "Michael is the one you're saying is the realistic one?"

Montaviel continued, "Yes, very realistic. Maybe not the preferential choice, but we weren't looking at this as a preferential choice. We were looking at a realistic experience that needed to happen within a certain time frame. Bingo. It happened. It's not a coincidence. It's our job. Alavan and Brent chuckled. "But now, your choice brings a new realistic or unrealistic experience. It's your choice. To see how far we can stretch your imagination. To see how far you stretch your reality to form a new one. Not to see how unrealistic we can become, but to see how real we are as people. We aren't as limited as we think. We are only limited by the limitations we place on ourselves. No more than that. No less than that. Simple. Too simple. For a limited mind, for limited expression. Does it have to be complex? There has to be more truth in that, surely. No, it's too easy. That's why we don't get it. It's too easy. It's no big hocus pocus. It's all right there and it's always been right there. You are who you are because of the experiences you've had. Not because of the emotions you place in the experience. Just the experience itself. The emotion is separate. The feeling is separate. Every experience is powerful. Very powerful. And it needs to be. Some experiences are uncomfortable to show you the wholeness of who you are. We can't show you the wholeness of who you are through pleasurable things. We can't. Anybody that goes through life wearing blinders thinking that everything is just the most glorious thing and nothing's ever gone wrong in their life, has never experienced life. That's all I have to say about that."

Alavan said, "And the human body doesn't even do that. It has both."

Montaviel replied, "Always both at the same time, continuously. Automatically. Always. It's not the way we would like it to be sometimes, but it's the way it is."

Montaviel closes his eyes and appears to be thinking.

"Uncomfortable to me is... Uncomfortable is a miracle. Uncomfortable is a miracle; not waiting to happen, but the uncomfortability of the experience is the miracle happening. It's a miracle to have that happen. Think of the alternative of not having an experience at all. The alternative is nothing. Nothing happens because we want to play it safe. Because we don't want to hurt. We don't want to hurt so we don't experience. So, we go through life with blinders on. Most people do that to some extent, depending on how large their blinders are. And they will experience that time and time again."

Montaviel continued, "It's not unrealistic or unreasonable for Spirit to think that a life form can achieve everything it needs to achieve in a single life. It's happened many times, but because of the limitations you place upon yourself, you don't want it to happen. So, it's your choice how many times you want to go through it. Doesn't matter to us. Keeps us working."

A Higher Channel

Alavan and Brent laughed. "We always have a job. But if it wasn't you, I'd be with someone else. So, I'm part of you. I'm part of the guidance that places these obstacles here. Trivan (Brent's 5th-dimensional spirit) doesn't like obstacles as much. He tries to make the obstacles a little bit easier to overcome. I place them there. He covers them up. That's his job." Montaviel smiled. "But that's what he's there for. And if you look at the coexistence of that energy together, it works perfectly. I place them, he covers them, and you ignore them. It works perfectly." Brent and Alavan laughed.

Alavan asked, "He doesn't feel bad about it?"

Montaviel replied, "Of course not, it's his job. It's his job to cover up what I put there. And it's your job to look the other way. Everybody's working together. We all stay working. You start looking and I will have to find another job. I can keep doing it for a long time."

Brent asked, "If I start looking for…"

Montaviel replied, "If you start looking at the obstacles as real, oh, I've got to work a little bit faster." Montaviel smiles

Alavan asked, "I don't want to get too far off the subject, but when was the last time you were in form?"

Montaviel said, "18,000 years ago."

Chapter 6: Giving Up All Emotion

Somé, Paige, and I signed up for the April walk-in event in San Raphael with Savizar and Silarra, the same walk-ins we saw in Sedona, Arizona. Since we were all living together, we could tell if someone wasn't feeling right emotionally or mentally. Somé seemed to be struggling with everything that was happening to him, and he said his emotions were just too strong. He was really upset. He said he could sense how other people were feeling, which brought on his own emotions. Between that and all the thoughts coming to him, it was very difficult to deal with, especially because it was all so new. He said the emotions were so strong and uncontrollable that he would rather die than go on. I couldn't fathom what he must be going through. We went for a walk in the neighborhood, trying to find some peace and relaxation for Somé. The event was the next day, and I suggested he focus on taking deep breaths and hoping that a good night's sleep might be refreshing.

The next morning, Somé returned from a walk and said he barely slept a wink, having been so emotional all night, crying endlessly. It was all just so overwhelming for him, and his emotional body was completely freaking out. He felt like he had lost control of everything inside him, and his hands were shaking. We also felt helpless to help him as there is no manual for this sort of thing. We began to question if a road trip was even a good idea right now. He said he wanted to go but just needed to gather himself. I didn't have much confidence that things would improve.

A bit later, he called me over and said he was asking Spirit to take his emotion because he just couldn't deal with it. I told him that it was insane—that our emotion is part of who we are, and you can't just take it away. He said, "I can't go on like this. I have no other choice." I insisted, "Yes, you do. We can work through this." I couldn't comprehend what someone would be like without emotion, but I knew Somé was very emotional. He loved gardening, classical music, being a father, and had a recent relationship that broke his heart. It was a younger man, a hairdresser, who told Somé that he loved him but just needed some money to get his salon going in Los Angeles. Of course, Somé did what he could to help, but in the end, the guy just strung him along until Somé was fed up, heartbroken, and finally quit supporting and seeing him.

Somé was sitting on his bed with his head in his hands, sobbing. He kept saying, "I can't go through this. They said they could take my emotion, but there's a chance I can't come back. That's okay." Then, suddenly, his hands lowered to his side, his head came up, the somber look was completely gone, and he just said, "Let's go."

I wasn't sure what had just happened, so I had to ask, "Go where?"

He said, "To the event."

I asked, "How do you feel? You were sobbing a minute ago, saying that you couldn't go on."

He replied, "No, I didn't. I'm ready to go. Let's go." This was truly bizarre. I didn't know what had just happened.

I told Paige that he seemed fine, had no recollection of being upset, and was ready and eager to go to the event. He even wanted to drive. What a complete turnaround. Did it work? Did they remove his emotion? Is it reversible? How would he act now that his feelings were gone? I guess we were about to find out. I was completely confused and uneasy about the whole thing. How was this even possible?

We all loaded into my 1979 Honda Accord hatchback. It's a small car but can easily fit four people. Plus, it had a cassette player, and I remembered to grab a cassette for Somé: *Mozart's Greatest Hits*, including his favorite piece, "Piano Concerto No. 21."

There was an eerie silence as we closed the doors, and Somé started the car. He was already familiar with the car, having driven it before, and he pulled out of the driveway quickly. I thought this couldn't be a new spirit he was channeling because he acted like himself, except everything had this quickness about it—his moves, reactions, and driving. His driving was quite aggressive, and I remember asking him to slow down. I asked why he was driving so fast, and he replied, "This is how I always drive." But it wasn't. He would normally exceed the speed limit occasionally, but now there was seeming impatience. However, he showed no emotion about anything. I asked if he knew where he was going. He said, "Yes, we talked about taking Highway 1 up through San Francisco." That was correct.

That's exactly what we had discussed, but he seemed so different now. Cold even.

As we made our way up the highway, I asked, "Do you remember what happened just before we left?"

"We got ready and then we left," he replied.

"You don't remember being upset uncontrollably and wanting to get rid of your emotions?" I asked.

"No, why would I want to do that? It doesn't make any sense," he answered matter-of-factly. He had no recollection at all of feeling overwhelmed or emotional about anything. I couldn't believe this was happening.

As we drove past Aptos, where he had built a life with his ex-wife and five kids, I asked if he remembered what went on there. He said he felt a connection but had no actual memories. What? I reminded him that he had raised five children there with his ex-wife. He just shrugged.

The next 30 minutes felt tense in the car, and it was very quiet as I collected my thoughts. Paige wasn't saying anything, but I felt there was no way we could go on like this—it was like he had an emotional lobotomy. It was not the Somé we knew before. I figured I needed to reset the conversation.

"Do you consider yourself spiritual?" I asked.

"Yes," he responded.

"Do you remember hearing all those thoughts in your head and channeling Zitron and Botra?"

"I remember talking with you two about the events and hearing what was said after the fact, yes."

"Do you remember having all those random thoughts as well?"

"Yes."

"Do you remember how it made you feel?"

"I don't think it made me feel anything in particular," Somé said. He was the same person, just without all that emotion. He didn't sound like a robot, but he was very matter-of-fact, which made him seem like a different person.

We spent the next hour or so having small conversations and stopped along the coast at a turnout to take in the view of the ocean. There were low-hanging clouds over the ocean with spots where the sun was peeking through. It was a beautiful sight. I asked Somé if it made him feel anything. He said it was beautiful but didn't make him feel anything specific. Wow. I started to tear up. This man was made from emotion before. It was everything about him. It was how he connected to people, plants, and everything. It defined who he was. And he just threw it away. This cannot and should not be allowed to happen, I thought, not like this.

A Higher Channel

As we got back into the car to finish our trip to San Rafael, I thought we should continue the conversation about what happened and what we might do next. But I knew one thing for sure: we couldn't ignore that a critical part of Somé had vanished into thin air.

I started explaining to him what happened in the days, weeks, and moments leading up to his identity shift. He said it wasn't possible—that a spirit would never do that. It was interesting that this version of himself could have that kind of clarity and knowledge about what a spirit might do or not do but no memory of the emotional distress he was under just hours ago. Spirit must have removed that memory for this process to take hold. I continued recounting the events, but he didn't seem to believe it. Paige was indifferent. It seemed she was okay with the new version of him. I think she preferred it—somehow less of a threat or something. She kept telling me to just leave things alone, but I couldn't do that.

Our conversations continued until we reached the Bed and Breakfast, where we had reservations. As we pulled into the parking lot, Mozart's "Piano Concerto No. 21" was ending, and as we stopped, he asked me, "What usually happens to me when I listen to this music?" I answered, "You are normally so moved emotionally that you would spot your pants," I said, nodding toward his groin. As we both looked down, it was clear that the body still felt the emotion even though Somé had been disconnected from the feeling. It was as if something sank in at that point, and he realized everything I had been saying was true. He looked at me with understanding and said, "I see now."

We checked in and made our way to our room, which had a very antique theme. The beds could've been from the 30s or 40s, but they seemed comfortable enough. There was a common bathroom on the floor. "So, this is what bed and breakfasts are like," I thought.

We gathered in the room, and I asked Somé if he had any new thoughts about what had happened and if we should ask Spirit to reverse it. He replied that nobody should give up an important core part of who they are. Paige said to leave it the way it was and was defiant. I continued to press.

"Can you ask them to reverse it?" I asked. He said, "They said that if we are going to do it, we have to do it now."

I replied, "If the body can survive, do it!"

He said, "There's never a guarantee, but they will start now." His head lowered, and he began mumbling in another language. Then, suddenly, he grabbed his head and slowly lowered it again. He started crying and sobbing with his head down. He slowly raised his head and opened his eyes, tears streaming down his face.

"Are you okay?" I asked.

"Yes," he nodded. I asked if he remembered what happened. He said he remembered the trip and our conversations.

"How do you feel now? Are your emotions back? Are they at the same intensity as before?" I asked.

"Yes, they are back, but I don't feel overwhelmed like I did before. I'm not sure what changed, but something has."

"Maybe they helped with the intensity and the helpless feeling?" I suggested.

"Maybe," he said and added, "I do feel like me again." I asked if he was hungry or needed to rest, and he opted for a bite to eat. They had some snacks downstairs, so we went to check them out. Paige, on the other hand, did not seem happy about what had transpired.

We had a snack and then a little nap before heading over to the event. Somé wanted Zitron to attend the event. I asked if he had the strength for that, and he said he asked Spirit, and they said they would not do it if his form was at risk. But it was important for Somé, so he brought Zitron along. The seminar lasted about two hours. Much of the talk was about things we had heard before—the expansion of the energies in and around the planet, expanding our own realities, and co-creating heaven on earth. I wondered if they could tell that he was channeling. Savizar acknowledged Somé and Zitron, saying, "I see we have someone co-creating Heaven on Earth right here. Welcome."

Zitron responded with a simple "Thank you." It was short and sweet, but Somé was happy to be acknowledged. It all went so fast. I was mind-blown by the events of that day and what we had experienced. It seemed like they knew but didn't want to make a big deal of it. Besides, they were walking channels themselves.

After the event, we stopped at a Mexican food restaurant, ordered dinner, and had margaritas for all! We were flying high. Well, except Paige. She seemed to be just getting through everything. We loaded back into the car and discussed the event. I was in the driver's seat, Paige in the passenger seat, and Somé in the back. His elbows were resting on our bucket seats, and he was perched forward a bit as we all talked. I don't know what I was thinking, maybe I wasn't thinking at all when I leaned over and gave him a prolonged kiss on the lips. I was just feeling the vibe of the moment, glad that he was going to be okay, not really considering the impact it might have on someone else. Paige blew up, shouted some expletives, asked how I could do such a thing, got out of the car, and started walking down the street. I chased after her, apologized, and pleaded with her to get back into the car. She finally did but was still very mad at me. It was a quiet ride back to the B&B.

Paige was upset when we returned and said that Somé needed to get his own room. I checked, but the front desk said they were full. Somé said he was just going to sleep outside on the bench. I continued to apologize to Paige and said we couldn't just leave him outside on the bench. After a couple of hours, she acquiesced, and I went and asked Somé to return to the room.

The ride back was quiet. I tried to patch things up with Paige over the next couple of weeks, but I also made it clear to her that I didn't want to end my friendship with Somé. She ended up moving out shortly thereafter.

Back to the San Francisco session with Brent.

Montaviel sensed from Brent's reaction that the session was about to end. However, it felt as though things were not quite resolved. Montaviel decided to stay, stating that it was important to finish what they started.

Brent admitted, "You know, I don't know about things like this..."

"I don't either," Montaviel responded.

Brent continued, "It's nice to have Alavan here to ask questions as well. I realize that I have a natural tendency to stop talking when I'm uncomfortable."

"That's not a natural tendency; that's a reality you have," Montaviel said. "When something doesn't fit into your limited perspective, you stop. It doesn't mean this reality is less or more significant than any other. When you reach a point where you can't absorb more information, you turn off, you stop. My initial remark after the video camera went off was to imply that I was trying my best to expand your reality by letting you experience something longer than you would have allowed yourself. I'm here to give you a different perspective, a different reality, a different feeling. You're not listening to someone else; you're listening to yourself.

"It's easy to see a different form and face, but hard to comprehend that this is you. This is every thought you've had, every thought you wanted. This is your every desire, right here. And I know more about you than what this face and form reveal to you in your reality."

Brent, puzzled, asked, "But why is it so difficult to accept what I just experienced and move on? If this is me, why is it so hard to accept it as an experience? If I know that's the way it should be because I'm sitting here saying if Alisal could be back tomorrow morning, it would be so easy."

"Exactly," Montaviel replied. "I am an expanded expression of the reality you can't comprehend. You get glimpses, looks, and feelings. That's all I've been able to offer until you're ready to ask for more. But don't ask for anything you're not willing to accept the consequences for. Don't ask if there's too much fear within you to accept what life has to offer. It's much easier for me. Triven has a better job. I have less to do," Montaviel smiled.

Alavan interjected, "There are also parts of him that could be talking to him, saying, 'Oh, I know exactly how you feel. I feel the same way. I agree with you 100%.'"

"Yes, support systems," Montaviel acknowledged.

"So, you're saying you're not the only part of him?" Alavan asked.

"I'm a small part, a very small part," Montaviel confirmed.

Brent inquired, "Are you saying the next 40 years will be like last year or worse?"

Montaviel asked, "Under what reality are you forming this opinion?"

"Well, you said that if I make the choice, Alisal will be back tomorrow," Brent replied.

"Yes," Montaviel affirmed.

"And I would have 40 years of what I had, or am I making things worse for myself?" Brent wondered.

Montaviel said. " What you had this past year is exactly what you had. Don't expect any more or any less. Only in your own reality can more be gained. But that experience holds no more than what you've already got. If you want it to last 20 years, it can. Want to try for 60? We can do 60 years. How about 72 and three-quarters? We can extend it as long as you want. But that's not the point. The point is that you already know what the experience holds. You know every in and out and possibility of what you went through. You know all the glory and the living hell. It can't be any more than that. But it can last if you want it to. Press a few buttons, make a few calls; it's easy."

Alavan thought for a moment before speaking. "I think he believed there could have been more in that experience."

Montaviel shook his head. "No. The experience you and Somé had—one moment of that experience—is equal to the existence of his entire lifetime here on earth. No more, no less. One moment. The glorious feeling of one moment. Probably a week ago last month, besides the original May 5th, was one of the greatest moments Spirit's had to offer you. It's the greatest experience you were able to have. Now, if your relationship lasted 20 years, would it diminish the feeling of that one moment a week ago last Monday? Can't you go on longer or shorter with these experiences? It lasted a few moments, but it holds a lifetime of feeling. Is the experience diminished because it only lasted a few moments? We can sit and lament that it has to last longer, but that's not necessary."

"But why did Somé want them to stay together?" Alavan asked.

Brent looked at Montaviel, his curiosity piqued. "That's what I want to know. Can you, could you ask Somé now?"

"That's why I'm asking someone who knows more than I do," Alavan interjected.

Montaviel explained, "It's a limited expression built-in to make you believe in what you have. When something feels good, you want it to last. It's part of who you are."

"Now, whether or not it supports our wholeness, is that a different issue?" Alavan asked.

Montaviel responded, "That has nothing to do with it. It can, but it doesn't. It can, and it could. What do YOU want to place upon that? How much of that experience do you want to place upon it? How much time does it take to experience an emotion? One second. How much time did it take you to experience a feeling? One second.

"So, we draw it out," Alavan said.

Montaviel nodded. "Because in your expression, you want to draw out anything that feels good. Why not? Why have it any less? But it doesn't hold any more meaning. It's just a built-in mechanism to keep you moving in one direction. Whether that direction is realistic or not doesn't matter. It's a mechanism to keep you moving. At the same time, you think you're moving, but you might be standing still, going nowhere, doing nothing from our perspective. This is the limitedness you place upon yourself versus the expansiveness of what's out there to experience. Yet you deny your own existence by limiting your experience. Tell ME why. Why is this something you find enjoyable to do?"

Montaviel continued, "I don't understand that. Not from my perspective now. I understand the desire for the feeling. I also understand that feeling comes in many forms. The feeling can come from many places. It just happened that this feeling came from one face."

Brent hesitated. "Am I wrong to..."

Montaviel interrupted. "No. You're not wrong. There's nothing wrong about anything. But why do you think that the emotion and the absence of this person diminishes the experience? Why does it have to mean 'it's over'? It's the beginning. It's the beginning of something new you were able to feel and experience."

"Okay," Brent said.

Montaviel smiled. "It's beautiful."

Brent asked, "Could this be a new reality if that other person decides to make an effort and change to include that person again?"

"Of course," Montaviel replied. "'Could' is a very expansive word in your limited sense of expression."

Brent laughed. "Yeah, I could be 99 years old and decrepit, and suddenly he would come back in."

Montaviel chuckled. "Well, now that's a whole new reality we can work on, isn't it? Talk about expansiveness! But what do we do for the next 99 years?"

"I'm sorry, I didn't mean to get sarcastic there," Brent said, chuckling.

"It wasn't directed at me," Montaviel reassured. "It was directed at yourself. What you say, what you feel, how you think doesn't diminish my presence because I'm always there," he said, pointing at Brent. "Right there is where I am."

Montaviel continued, "I'm showing you a side of yourself that knows exactly where your direction lies and will sit patiently, diligently, ever-present right there. The moment we feel a true thought come through—a thought you truly believe more than you can imagine—it happens instantly. So, the power of your thoughts and the intensity of your emotions are known instantaneously, and you're provided with exactly what you asked for under your guise of reality, under your limited expression. This is all we have to work with. We can't work with the expansiveness of what reality really is. We have to work with your limited expression."

Brent pondered, "But what would happen if that were the case? What would happen to the other person's reality?"

"Nothing. What do you mean what happens to the other person's reality?" Montaviel asked.

"Because that's not what the other person wants. If what I truly want is to have Alisal back as my partner, what happens to his reality if he has no choice in the matter?" Brent clarified.

"Oh, you mean if they force him to be there," Alavan interjected.

Brent asked, "He's saying that he'll place him right there at that moment. But what happens to his reality?"

"We change it. Instantly," Montaviel replied. "He could go over there tonight, and we'd have him back in your house by tomorrow morning. All

I have to say to Somé is, 'He's going back,' and you'd have him back there tomorrow."

Brent stammered, shaking his head slowly.

Montaviel continued, "We won't talk about the personal part of what he would go through by doing that, but would he do it? Oh, you bet. If Botra (Somé's 10th-dimensional spirit) came through and said, 'We have to do this now,' there's no one stopping him. He'll take them by the hand, and will he go? Oh, you bet he will. There's no way he can say no. No way. Will he believe under his limited reality? Absolutely. He will believe it, accept it, and do it. That's how easy it is to get things done when you choose. Very easy. Nothing hard about it."

Brent, still puzzled, asked, "But why does it seem that by making this choice, I'm putting a stop to any growth at all?"

Montaviel explained, "It depends on what reality you're coming from and what growth you're talking about. Are you talking about growth in spirituality, growth within your wholeness, or growth within the third-dimensional realm? There's a lot of growth in the third-dimensional realm you haven't experienced yet that you can still experience in this life. A lot. What reality base do you want to work on?"

"Why can't we grow from the same things?" Brent asked. "We had the same issues that we're working on. Why can't we do this together? Why do I have to experience it with somebody else?"

A Higher Channel

Montaviel responded, "Why can't you choose a different experience? Because you don't want to? Because you don't feel it's part of what..."

"Because I want to experience it with this person. And I'm putting the face on it. I know I am," Brent interjected.

"Exactly," Montaviel affirmed. "And nobody says you don't have to. You can put his face on it. You can put his face, his smell, his touch, everything on it. I'm just telling you that the choice is not unrealistic. It's realistic under a very third-dimensional realm of thinking. Very realistic. Very easy. And it can be done."

Chapter 7: New Beginnings

Things were moving fast. Somé was getting random thoughts from Spirit about dimensions and higher spirits that we all have. He could also sense and get information about other people. He said he could feel energies not only in his own body but also in others. He wondered if he could help others with his newfound gift.

As he got used to all this new information, there were times when he would channel little Somé or Zitron and let them hang out while he "stepped aside" and observed. One such day was in April 1990 when we went to the store and then out for a meal. Little Somé was first. He was a handful, a completely child-like spirit, constantly giggling and getting into things. On the drive, he pushed every button on the radio, twisted every knob on the heating controls, and raised and lowered the air vents multiple times. The visor and window crank were on a whole other level. Clearly, he had never seen this stuff before, and the world was his oyster.

I had to pop into a drugstore quickly and wondered if I could leave him alone in the car without him getting out and wandering around. I asked him if he understood the rules. He said he did. So, I told him the rule was that he had to stay in that seat while I went into the store. He said he understood. Then he asked if we could have sex. I wasn't sure where he got that word, but I said we could not because there are laws, bigger rules, that we must follow here on Earth. I reinforced that he had to stay in the seat, then ran into the store, got what I needed, and ran back out. Whew! He was still in his seat—although he had undone the seatbelt, wrapped it around himself several times, and around the gearshift. I didn't see how productive this was, so I asked him to get Zitron, which he did. I can say this—little Somé knows how to follow the rules. LOL!

With Zitron present, we headed to a local restaurant in a little shopping center. As we exited the car and walked towards the restaurant, we passed two elderly women. Zitron commented, "That's Barbara—she's having difficulties with her family." "Seriously?" I responded. As we passed them, I said, "Barbara" out loud, and one of them turned around. I apologized for mistaking her for someone else. She looked at me funny, and we continued to the restaurant. This was an example of how thin the veil is between us, our minds, and our thoughts. If you are in tune, you can pick up thoughts from just about anywhere, much like a radio.

As we sat down, it was clear that Zitron was also unfamiliar with modern conveniences. He looked at the utensils, and I explained that we use them to eat. I could tell Somé was talking to him as he would nod or turn his head slightly as if listening to what Somé was saying. He reached for a small plate with a couple of pats of butter wrapped in foil. I moved the plate closer to him, and he picked up a pat of butter, put the whole thing in his mouth, and began to chew it. I laughed and told him that's not the typical way we eat butter. I ordered food for both of us, Somé returned, and we finished our meal.

A Higher Channel

A couple of days later, I was in the health food store stocking shelves when a woman with striking gray hair approached me and said, "Hi, I'm Carol. I'm having a spiritual session in a couple of nights if you want to join us." This was completely bizarre because I'd never seen her before in my life. She seemed nice and genuine, and considering that my life now bordered on the bizarre, I said, "Okay." She then replied, "Bring your friend," and handed me a piece of paper with her address on it. How did she know about Somé? I had no idea what this spiritual session would entail. I thought to myself, this is either going to get really weird, really cool, or both. Wow, things are happening pretty quickly, I thought. There are other people out there with similar gifts, like Somé. And they live in the area!

A few nights later, we showed up at this house nestled on a wooded hill between Monterey and Carmel. We knocked on the door, and someone greeted us and led us to the living room, where Carol sat in a chair facing us. There were a couple of other people there as well, seated in a semi-circle. She thanked us for coming and said she would start shortly, as the spirits were already communicating with her. We had no idea what this was about or why we were there, but it seemed very relevant to what Somé was going through, so our interest was piqued.

Carol closed her eyes and said she could feel the presence of several spirits, especially one with a very large, wide presence. She said an amazing process was going to happen on May 5th (just a couple of weeks away) in the canyon behind our house, and it would involve all of us living there. It would be a very transformative process for one person. She pointed at Somé to indicate that he would be the focal point and said this process would expand Somé's awareness and capabilities. It was to make way for what he would do in the future. This process was very special and rarely happened, but it was to aid in the expansion of the energies at play right now. "This is your message," she said, "you are to prepare for this event starting very early, and it will last all day." We thanked her for her time and would never see her again. Some people come into your life for a short time but have a big impact. This was one of those moments.

As we drove home, we talked about how the reference to a large spirit must have been Botra. Somé asked Zitron, who confirmed that it was indeed Botra. So why not just have Zitron or Botra deliver the message directly? Zitron said it was because of the realities at play. Somehow it had more weight or value because it came from a different source. It also lent some validity to what Somé was going through to encounter someone else with similar experiences and capabilities. Sometimes the message we need can come from anywhere or anyone.

In the days that followed, we got even more details about how to prepare. Somé relayed that we should drink tea made from the bark of an oak tree to aid healing and prepare the mind for expansion. It just so happened that we had such a tree in the backyard. In fact, the house we were renting in Pebble Beach had a fairly good-sized backyard that backed up to a small canyon covered in trees, shrubs, and large ferns. We often had families of deer grazing, coming up from the canyon.

Spirit explained that we were going back in time, literally. Well, for Somé anyhow. They were going to take him back through each of his lifetimes and reconcile his experiences somehow. He would step through each one, followed by a period of rest or sleep. They said we couldn't have anything on our body that looked modern, as it would confuse Somé. They said that they would ensure that our blankets and foot coverings would be familiar to him, as would our faces and the wedding ring of his own that he could not remove. He would recognize us as tribe members or family.

We fashioned footwear from an old rolled-up carpet. We cut them big enough to tie around our ankles with the fuzzy part next to our skin. We had acrylic blankets since none of us could wear clothes. We also carried a basket of fruit that he would recognize as our sustenance for the day. When we made our way back to the house at the end of the day, he would not see it. None of us knew what to expect, but we were ready. Edmond and Angie, our roommates, would take turns using a rented camera to film the event. Batteries didn't last long back then, so they would have to film from a distance, zoom in when necessary, and run batteries back and forth. That left me, Somé, and another woman from the store where we worked who was game to be involved. We needed three core people to form an energetic triangle. This would also come into play later when Somé would be doing energy work to move disembodied spirits "into the light."

A Higher Channel

The actual process started the night before, on May 5th, with Zitron at the helm. But what we affectionately call "the caveman event" started around 6 am the next day. We donned our makeshift shoes, blankets, and fruit and headed down into the lush fern grotto behind our home, not knowing what was about to happen. It was just past 6:00 am, and it was light enough to see our way down there. A light mist, typical of Monterey Bay, filled the air. It was cool and a little damp, but our blankets and makeshift shoes kept us warm enough. Birds had just begun to chirp, and a lone crow cawed nearby. Zitron slowly led the way to find the perfect spot that would provide enough cover and serve as a realistic backdrop for reliving the early days of human life.

Zitron found a good place to lay Somé down and asked us to lie down near him. He covered up with a blanket, and we did the same. He asked that we not speak English for the next six hours or until the process was over. The day before, Botra had said we needed a word to pause the process if something went wrong. I thought for a second and said, "Phoenix," as it relates to rebirth from ashes. I wasn't sure what could go wrong, but we had neighbors on the other side of the canyon and a golf course nearby. Plus, I didn't really know how this process would play out.

A few minutes after Zitron/Somé lay down, his body began to twitch under the blanket. He awoke a few minutes later, and it was clear it was no longer Zitron but someone else. He slowly sat up, mouth slightly open, and looked around at his surroundings, slowly. At this point, he didn't see anything but the trees and ferns. He didn't notice anyone was around him yet. His head then dropped, and he slowly fell forward and then back up again. He was hunched over, still in his blanket. Then he raised his head, and just as he started looking around, his head went back down, and his body convulsed again for a few seconds before collapsing on his side. We later understood that each one of these episodes was an earlier lifetime. Moments later, he was awake again, sat up, and began looking around. He got low to the ground, made sure he was covered up, looked at me, and uttered something I didn't understand, so I answered with a grunt, unsure of what to say.

He began digging through the leaves and dirt on the ground as if looking for edible roots or something. He often looked up when a crow cawed, or a woodpecker worked on a nearby tree. He finally found the basket of fruit, smelled the fruit, and so I followed suit. He tore open an orange and ate the wedges. He then threw the remainder of each peel to me with a grunt as if sharing with me. He inspected a banana, opened it, and realized the fruit was inside. Sniffing the peel and then the fruit, he set them both down and reached for the bunch of bananas. Tossing each of us a banana, he wanted to make sure the rest of the tribe had something to eat as well.

Then he began inspecting his body. He tapped his shin, looked at his arm, and tugged at the hair on his arm and head. He then covered his head, lay down, and seemed to fall asleep for a short time before waking up again, this time acknowledging me with a couple of grunts. He moved closer to me and started rummaging through the ferns and ground. His blanket seemed to intrigue him as well—the pattern of sleeping, convulsing, waking, eating fruit, and rummaging repeated. Sometimes, the convulsing would happen while he was awake, his body freezing, then convulsing violently before collapsing, only to wake again a few moments later. I tried to mimic some of his movements and sounds to bring comfort to the situation. His exploration of roots became more vigorous with each iteration of life, as did his overall alertness. He often shook his head as if something inside was bothering him. He frequently pointed toward the sky or gestured upward. At one point, he kept motioning toward the camera and grunting. I think he saw the red light or something, so we signaled to Edmund to move away from that location.

If each nap was a lifetime, then he had been through about ten or so at this point. He was still crouched when he woke up, and food was always the primary concern. He started to stand around eleven or twelve o'clock to get a better look at his surroundings, then crouched again and covered up. He stood for the first time and walked to relocate the camp, moving about 15 feet closer to the center of the canyon but still covered in ferns. After we relocated, he smelled our hair, and we returned the favor. He looked up, and we looked up, continuing to mimic his actions.

He walked further into the canyon, holding his blanket around him to check out the surroundings. Nothing seemed amiss, so he settled down again to make a new camp. Convulsions started, and he grunted loudly, then collapsed. I heard him utter words that I couldn't understand, but he kept repeating them. I didn't know if he was conscious or not. He woke up and started motioning toward his head, pointing to it repeatedly. I had to assume the work Spirit was doing must be giving him a severe headache. All the convulsions alone in about an hour's time would give anyone a headache.

He looked at me and then up at the sky. His head shook a few times, and then he returned to looking up into the upper canyon. Some of the noises seemed strange to him. At one point, we heard a large machine, possibly some landscape equipment, out in the distance. He was very startled, and we tried to comfort him as best we could. He was scared, so he put his head down and covered up. I think he slept on and off for about 15 minutes. He woke up at one point, sounding unsure of what was happening, repeating something I didn't understand. He kept pointing to his head and then covered up again. He woke up moaning like he was in pain and then fell unconscious again. Sometimes the sleep was accompanied by tremors, sometimes not. At one point, he woke up, cried loudly toward the sky, and raised both hands as if to say, "Why, why?" and then grasped his head with both hands before falling back to the ground. He was trying to explain how his head felt and how he didn't know what was happening to him by gesturing, sobbing, and looking at the sky. Fast forward three hours later. I couldn't say how many lifetimes he had been through at this point, but I would guess 20 to 25.

A Higher Channel

He now stood up straight, wrapped the blanket around him like a toga but left a shoulder exposed, and surveyed the area. He was much more confident. He seemed to be leading us and was clearly the commander of the group. We were all standing now. He tapped his heart and felt his head, mumbling something. As he looked around, he saw a potential pathway that led up toward the house (although it wasn't visible). He saw the camera again and said something to me, which I echoed. He then led us back into the ferns to find some protection. I motioned for Edmund to find a better spot higher up for the camera.

A few more naps and two hours later, the convulsions had lessened greatly, and he was on his feet again with the toga wrap and the basket of fruit. He wanted to venture to higher ground. He led the way slowly through the canyon, stopping occasionally to gather himself. Once he reached the base of the hill that led to our backyard, he was forced to stop as the tree canopies and brush thickened. His blanket fell off as he lost his footing, but he kept hold of it and the fruit basket and continued to march up the hill naked and unabated. He fell once but kept his pace. It seemed he was destined to reach the top, even if he didn't know what was up there. It was like a natural pull of destiny. The camera was behind us at this point, but Edmund made his way up using an alternate route so he could film us arriving at the top.

We arrived at a plateau and a clearing of sorts, although we were still among trees. We could see in front of us and all around. We were being filmed from the top of the hill now. Somé froze as Edmund got too close. He then moved to a cluster of trees and sat down with a worn look on his face as he ran his hands over his head. He was clearly still undergoing something that affected his mind and body, and it was confusing to him. He continued to try to talk to me, but because I didn't speak the language, I couldn't fully understand him. He seemed okay with this because he carried on and didn't seem to fault me for it. It was now 2:18 pm local time, a good seven hours and 20 minutes since this process began. The sun beamed down on us through the trees, and he tried to get up but couldn't, content to be receiving the relief the sun's rays provided. He began to speak, then closed his eyes, and tremors took over his body. His head shook from side to side gently for a few seconds. He jolted forward, waking up from this brief episode, and looked around quickly as if he knew someone or something was nearby. His fears were quickly allayed as he realized there was no imminent danger, and he surveyed his immediate surroundings once again. Looking up into the sun, then at his arms and legs, he repeated this discovery process each time he woke.

The cameraman behind us moved, and Somé mumbled something to me, indicating with a head movement that someone was nearby. He began slightly rocking back and forth and glancing over his right shoulder at the camera. He uttered very intense and direct words to me, indicating he knew someone was there and he was irritated by it. He made aggressive arm movements, indicating the stranger should move away or that we should leave. He continued to express his displeasure verbally as he wrapped his blanket around him, leaving one shoulder out, and stood up. He walked past the camera without looking at it, began walking up the hill, and then stopped. He looked back at where we were, and I noticed the fruit basket was still there. He nodded at it and said something, so I walked over and retrieved the basket. He then continued his march up the tree-lined hill with purpose. He took several steps, stopped abruptly, bent over, shook a little, and then stood straight up. He seemed to have a new identity as he looked around to survey the environment. He looked at me in my blanket, holding the fruit basket, then at himself in his blanket and makeshift shoes. He looked up the hill and around us, then took a deep breath—which I hadn't seen him do before. He looked at me again and, with a confident disposition, slowly proceeded up the grade through the forest. With the branches and dead leaves crunching under our feet, we moved slowly toward the top. He stopped at the base of a huge tree, and we sat down. He spotted Edmund again, grabbed a big stick, and started beating it on the ground. Just then, his eyes closed, and he started shaking. I sensed that Spirit must be intervening during these times when activities were close to escalating. I signaled to Edmund to move below us. He did, and Somé woke up again, stood up, motioned towards the top, and we started moving forward again. He stopped, looked backward, upward, and then at his arm. He clenched his fist, bent his arm, and looked at his bicep. He touched the fruit basket and began the ascent again. We were close to the house now, but it still wasn't visible. He stopped, bent down, shook, and as he rose up, he had a very soft look on his face. He gave me a sweet smile and pulled the blanket over most of his head. I realized that he was a woman at this point. She gazed at the path and the canyon from where we emerged, and we just stood there, taking in its beauty. She looked down at the basket and asked me something in a language I still didn't understand. Obviously, I couldn't answer her, so I just stood there. She repeated herself, then motioned toward the basket, and I realized she wanted me to pick it up. But then she saw the camera. She put her hand out and asked to see my hand, which I extended. She looked at both our hands, then turned away from the camera and toward the canyon. The other people who were with us earlier had gone back to the house, and I could hear a radio or someone talking in the house. Somé became startled and started running back down into the canyon. No, I thought, this can't be happening! Oh, wait, the safe word! As she started descending into the canyon, I yelled, "Phoenix!" and she stopped in her tracks. I went to her side and waited. She slowly started to move and opened her eyes. I couldn't tell if it was a male or female life at this point. We both stared up toward the house. It seemed to be male as he had the blanket back down around his shoulders and motioned for me to follow toward the house again. We got to the backyard, and there was someone talking on the phone. Somé had a look of consternation on his face, eyebrows furrowed. But I got him to sit down and face away from the house. He sat, bowing his head one last time, and he slept for a while. When he woke up, it was Zitron who said, "The process is over." Whew! I wasn't sure that we'd make it. Almost eight and a half hours had passed since we began at 6:45 am that morning.

It was 9:00 pm that night, and Zitron was still with us. I fired up the camera and asked him a few questions. I asked him what planet he was from, and he said, "Tekstar." He also said that both he and Botra are very happy that the process went well. I don't imagine they have any better way to explain it using our words. Montavien (Edmond) and Altura (Angie) (using their higher spirit names) helped us get through the process, as did our co-worker from the store. It was truly mind-blowing to witness and participate in such an event. I don't think we fully understood the impact, but it sounded like it would allow Somé to expand his capabilities going forward. I remember that night Zitron said he wanted to ensure that Somé had a clean body when he returned. So, I showed him where the soap and shampoo were and how to use them. Later, he brought Botra in, who told me they were going to let the body sleep for a while and that I had to wake him up at 11:00 pm sharp. If I didn't, there would be irreversible consequences. He also asked if they should change Somé's face. I said, "What do you mean?"

Botra replied, "We are aware of certain realities that prefer a certain look. We can make that change." I suddenly knew that he was talking about me and my perfectionist outlook, which I held so dearly (I shielded myself from almost all potential relationships). While it was an insecurity and defense mechanism, it certainly didn't need to be bolstered.

"No," I replied, "that's ridiculous." I felt like they were teaching me a lesson in acceptance and love. The 11:00 pm thing was another lesson to pay attention and focus (and not to fall asleep). They were coming at me hard, but sometimes intensity is required to crack a thick shield. It's also something that I will never forget.

I stayed awake while he slept and woke Somé up at 11:00 p.m. to ask if he remembered anything. He said he vaguely remembered a sharp pain in his head, but that was it. "Do you feel any different?" I asked him.

"Not right now – I can't tell. It feels like I just woke up." Truer words could not have been spoken.

Back to the San Francisco session.

Brent asked, "But does the world stop? Or is there still a possibility of growth?"

Montaviel replied, "Under what reality? What kind of growth?"

"Well, we both want spiritual growth," Brent said. "And we're in the third dimension. So, we have to grow third dimensionally. I think that's just... I mean..."

Montaviel interrupted, "What was so wonderful? I know your answer, but I want to hear you say it. What was so wonderful and so special in that one year? What was the most special part of it?"

"The most special part was having him there. The feeling of having him there," Brent answered.

"Thank you. Now, what was the worst part?" Montaviel asked.

"The worst part, I guess, was... can this be...the lack of feeling," Brent admitted.

Montaviel responded, "Thank you. Now, we agree on one thing: feeling. How can the worst and best feelings be associated with the same thing when you want to place a face on a feeling instead of the experience? In this experience, you're only thinking about the pleasurable moments you don't want to let go of. But equally and just as emotionally, the other part of that experience is also still there, and it only multiplies with time. It starts out slowly, becomes more, and becomes more. Why? Because in our mind, we multiply it and then ignore what we see. You know what it's like. You did it easily because you wanted one small part of the experience to go on and on. So, you create a wall between yourself and the uncomfortable part. The wall goes up. We don't see it, hear it, smell it, or taste it. The other person in that experience can become, in your terms, a living hell, the devil. He's wonderful. Look how nice his hair is. Look in his eyes. Oh, look at his cute butt. Look at this. Look at that. And yet we're looking at 'the devil' in action. But our reality and what we want to believe is the existence of beauty in this experience. Yes, it can hold that. But it also holds all these other parts. Where are YOU in this experience?" Montaviel pointed at Brent with both hands. "We know where everybody else is. Where are you? Where do you place yourself? And don't tell me it's been so long that you can't remember how you feel. I know how you feel."

Brent, frustrated, said, "I know."

A Higher Channel

"So, why can't we, just for the sake of thinking about something new, take that experience, that feeling, and that face and say it belongs to that face? Oh, yeah. I don't want to forget that face. The most beautiful face has this expression. But we also don't want to discredit that face with having the other emotion either. This face brought me the worst feeling I had and that I shouldn't have had in this relationship. But he brought it, and it was there. I experienced it. I felt it, and it hurt inside. It hurt to think that all of my being was put out and it was totally ignored. And in an instant, it was taken away. And in an instant, there was no more feeling. How can I put 100,000% of who I am into one small feeling, and have it totally ignored? I cannot imagine. That IS the existence of choice. And you have to know what the existence of choice means. And THAT'S what it means. This is the existence of choice. You choose, we deliver. Pickup and delivery." Montaviel laughed. "That's what it's all about. No more, no less. But you can STILL have everything you want, and you can have that face right there. Only under the reality that you're in, the present. Don't look for expanded realities within this limited expression. It can't come. Can't. Impossible. And there aren't many things that I will say are impossible.

"This one, yeah. But in the disguise of forming a new reality within our weak minds, we'll think of something. We really will. We'll think of something to disguise it, to make it okay. But where are you in all this?" Montaviel pointed to his body. "We never find you. You get lost and go through another life form, experiencing what you need to experience, gaining what you need to gain.

"And we know exactly how long each period is going to last. That's why your window is set at a certain time because we know how long it's going to take. So, this time we're spending right now has no bearing on any decision you're going to make or any thought you have at the moment because we already know. But it's your choice.

"It's your choice to do what you're going to do. We know what choice you're going to make. No doubt in our minds. We are as clear as the blue sky. But we know what you have to go through to get there. And it's not very pleasant. But we know where your choice is, just like a game we have to play. We know. We roughly know when it will happen, given a certain time frame. We know in what lifetime what goes on. We know how to plan. We know what obstacles to place there. And then you probably think, if it's all predestined and pre-planned, why do we have these obstacles there to try to change your mind? It's our job." Montaviel laughed.

Brent added, laughing, "And it's Triven's job to cover them up."

"It's our job," Montaviel continued. "But it's not relentless or meaningless. It's part of the expansiveness in creating new realities every moment. Whether you recognize it or not, your reality changes about 17,000 times daily. 17,000 times a day. A new way, twist, turn, up, down."

Alavan asked, "Would you call that a new experience?"

"It's not so much a new experience as a different reality within the same experience," Montaviel explained. "You can have the same experience in one lifetime a million times and yet have 50 different reality bases that you're working on. You don't work on one reality base at a time. Impossible. Brent probably works on about 16,000 different reality bases. On a daily basis, you, Alavan, work on about 200 different reality bases. Somé works on about 125. That's the average."

"125 is the average for most people on the planet?" Alavan asked.

"125 would be average for someone like Somé. The average for people on the planet now is about 15,000 to 16,000." Montaviel looked at Brent. "So, you're no better off or worse than anyone else."

"You know, I know quite a few," Montaviel continued. "We're talking about averages, highs, and lows. Having Somé brings that average down. But then there are forms walking around that you know of that we don't have to mention, carrying about 155,000 different reality bases right now. And you think, how can they think that fast? Well, they can."

"What's the low?" Alavan asked.

"What's the low? About 120."

"Nobody walks around with like three or four?" Alavan laughed.

"I can't see how that would be possible," Montaviel laughed along with Alavan and Brent.

"I don't know. That's why I'm asking you," Alavan said, still laughing.

"Think of all the higher spirits you have," Montaviel said. "All those realities right there."

"Yeah, right. Okay," Alavan replied.

"There are different realities based on the different ways you perceive life. At 120, you call the person a living saint," Montaviel added. "That's how your reality base would look at it. But I don't know if anybody has less than 120. Someone your Western culture emphasizes a lot, Christ, had 120 reality bases in that form, that way of thinking in the limitedness he was given. I can't see anybody operating with less than that because there's no way to keep your thinking straight. You need different ways to determine different realities and different ways of looking at things to decide what direction to take, what path to walk, and how to make your choices. They come from different reality bases. They don't just come from your higher spirits. They also come from outside sources. There's more outside influence that determines your choice than whatever I can get to you. A lot more. But not for Somé. It's the other way around. Why? Because he uses these things." Montaviel pointed to his ears. "He uses this thing." He pointed to his head. "He listens to this." He pointed to an ear and then his head. "So, his choices of reality bases have shrunk tremendously quickly.

"But he had to give it up to achieve what he wanted. The easiest way was from his heart. He told himself, "I can't do it by myself," and truly believed it. Every other possible reality faded, and it could end just like that. But that's when what he called "collapsing" happened.

Alavan asked, "How do you know when it happens? When we switch from using someone else's reality?"

Montaviel replied, "You know it, but you don't want to acknowledge it. You don't want to give it any credit. You trust yourself more in your choices. How people think and how they're wired to think makes you believe it's all your doing. But your part in it is just a tiny speck." He pointed to a speck on the table and laughed. "That's your contribution. That's all you have to offer. Everything else is pre-planned—energy forces, thoughts, the vast reality that Spirit has for you. It's endless," he said, opening his arms wide and mimicking looking into the distance. "Endless," he repeated with a laugh. "But our limited boxes keep us in our limited feelings, minds, and emotions, preventing us from experiencing what's already here for us to experience."

Montaviel continued, "Just make the choice. If you choose, I have something to do. If you don't, I sit back and listen. There's nothing wrong with that. I've been doing it for thousands of years. It's easy."

Alavan asked, "Do you get bored?"

Montaviel shook his head. "No. There's plenty to do. The expansiveness of thought works like your telephone. You press numbers, and it rings across the planet instantly. But I can do it faster. That's the power of thought. My thoughts can travel around the world and back in one second. One second. Bop, boom, done."

Alavan then asked, "What do you see when you're in spirit? I mean, we see in form. But when you're in spirit, what do you see? One thing? A million things?"

Montaviel replied, "I don't know what you expect in your limited form of reality."

Alavan, excitedly, said, "I don't know either. Do you see a planet with people, or are you in the sky looking down at it? Do you see forms everywhere?"

Montaviel replied, "You're limiting yourself here. We're talking about thought. Show me a picture of what thought looks like, and I'll show you a picture of us. In that thought form, we can acknowledge another thought being, another spirit. The acknowledgment of its presence, knowing it's there, is there. Expansive. That's my reality."

Alavan asked, "Is there space where there is no spirit?"

Montaviel said, "No. Show me a picture of thought with no space." He laughed.

Alavan nodded. "I guess it's really a third-dimension question." Montaviel looked toward the cigarettes. He picked one up, and Brent lit it for him.

Brent commented, "You're getting good at that."

Alavan said, "It's nice of you to come down and tread water with us."

Montaviel said, "Even these little sticks, what you call cigarettes, are incomprehensible in my experience. The reality that it takes for me to comprehend the usefulness and functionality of this is incomprehensible in my experience. Non-existent."

Alavan giggled and replied, "I'm sure you'd say the same for a million things down here."

Montaviel nodded. "For all the things. I can't find any useful things here."

Alavan asked, "Not clothing, not shelter?"

Montaviel shook his head. "No, because that's not you. I'm in the business of being you," he motioned toward Brent, who laughed. "I'm not in the business of being your cigarettes, your clothes, or your houses, or your cars. Those things just enhance the pleasure of your existence here."

Alavan asked, "So, our purpose here is to find ourselves?"

Montaviel replied, "There's no reference in 'you' as a spirit. You want it to, but it doesn't."

Brent said, "It gives pleasure to our form... Like companionship gives pleasure to my form but..."

Montaviel shook his head. "Nothing to do with you."

Brent repeated, "That has nothing to do with me?"

Montaviel shook his head again.

Alavan said, "Wouldn't you say it gives pleasure to the reality you hold? Because pleasure to the form is..."

Brent interrupted, "But we put so much emphasis on it. As John Bradshaw said, 'you cannot fulfill your existence here without another human being'."

Montaviel agreed, "Very true. Impossible. I've said that twice tonight. Impossible."

Alavan laughed and then asked, "Do we get into trouble when we qualify it? When we put a face on it and say it can only be this person?" Montaviel nodded but looked toward Brent.

Montaviel explained, "The experience ahead for this one here," he gestured toward Alavan, "is nothing like what he's going through now. If he fixes what this experience should look like in his mind, he can't experience what needs to happen."

Alavan said, "I had no clue. I feel so stupid sometimes. I think I couldn't even come close to..."

Montaviel interrupted, "That's why you have to open your eyes, your mind, your love, and your emotions to the experience. But don't let the experience be the only reason you feel that way. It has nothing to do with it. The experience is what you need to go through."

Alavan said, "That's where I get into trouble. Or I mean, that's what we do."

Montaviel replied, "It's the only thing you do. You place a different reality on the experience, making it different. I can take the same experience you're in now, give you a hundred realities to work from, and show you a hundred different ways of looking at it. We place too much emphasis on the experience being us. It's not us; it's just the experience. Don't give it more credit than it deserves. You're not the experience."

Alavan nodded. "That's what we do, don't we? We take our feelings and experiences and say, 'This is me. All of me.'"

Brent added, "When I was with Alisal, I felt closer to myself than ever before. I felt like I had something to offer."

Alavan asked, "Would you agree with him?"

Montaviel nodded affirmatively. "I agree."

Brent continued, getting emotional, "People saw so much of what I felt was me."

Montaviel explained, "And what brought out that feeling of you? I will tell you what brought out the feeling of you. The experience brought out the feeling of you. Not the face. The experience. Now, did this feeling just appear from nowhere? No, that's you. That's real. Don't diminish that within yourself. Don't beat yourself up about the experience."

Brent said, "I know, but why can't that experience continue?"

Montaviel responded, "Why can't you live for a thousand years? It's the same thing."

Brent said, "Because my physical form won't allow it."

Montaviel explained, "The choice you made won't let your physical form continue with the experience. If you made a different choice, you could live a thousand years. It might not make much sense, but we'd let you do it just like you choose to be with certain things. It's your choice. It's your limited expression that stops you from doing anything else. The choice is yours to have and keep forever. We won't deny anyone their choice. Never have, never will. But you have to know what reality you're using to make this decision."

Brent said, "I'm worried that the three people I care most about will look down on me for making the choice I want most in my life."

Montaviel replied, "That could never happen. Never."

Brent continued, "It's just something Somé said earlier. I think the choices I make could take them completely out of my life."

Montaviel agreed, "That's true. But in his expansive way of thinking, he's not putting an experience with the word 'choice.' You said 'choice,' but not what choice. The exact question was whether your choice could affect your relationship with those people now. Yes, it could. But you're not saying what the choice is. You have to be precise."

Brent clarified, "Okay. If I choose to be with Alisal for the rest of my life as a partner and work on our lives as best we can, will this diminish the relationship I have with Alavan, Somé, and Alisal?"

Montaviel replied, "In that question, no. But let's look at it from a different reality."

Brent agreed, "Okay."

Montaviel continued, "From their perspective, will it affect them? Yes. It has to. There's no other way. Cause and effect are driven by choices. Sure, it will affect them. Will it affect them in a way you see as positive? No, you won't see it as positive. It will be, but you won't see it that way. Remember, with your limited thinking, you're saying 'I,' placing yourself as your reality. If you do this, will it diminish how you feel and what happens with the relationship? No, because you will form another reality to offset what you see, to make it more comfortable. That's how we operate daily. But if you want to work on the reality of the wholeness of yourself, we're talking about something completely different."

Chapter 8: Guests Arrive

Somé switched into explorer mode at that point. He knew he could channel Zitron, Somé, and Botra, but he wondered if he could channel anyone else. He sent out an open invitation to any fifth-dimensional spirit. This was important because there are many disembodied spirits with different energies that might not align with our goal of embodying love and light. Living on Earth already gives us enough limited expression, repression, and challenges. Why invite someone who might bring more of that? A fifth-dimensional spirit would either be pure in essence (like little Somé) or understand the realities at play and represent love, honor, and light. We didn't know what to expect, but our new visitor was a hoot!

"Hiya, kid, got anything to drink?" Uh oh, I thought. Maybe this didn't work. "What kind of drink?" I asked. "The hard stuff, hooch, liquor, you know!" His tone and inflection made him sound like he spent a lot of time in the 30s and 40s. I said, "Sure, I think we have some beer in the fridge." I got the beer, opened it, and handed it to him. He seemed pleased just to hold it. "So, what brings me here?" He wasn't surprised to be here and seemed aware of how he got here. I explained that Somé was new to channeling and had already channeled a few higher spirits and was exploring his options. "Yes. I do something similar for someone I watch over. He doesn't like to go out alone but wants to experience nightlife, so he channels me, and we go out." I asked if this was happening today, which, in retrospect, was a silly question. I asked this spirit his name, and he said, "Tica" (pronounced tye-ka).

Oddly, as he was talking, I heard a bump at the front door. We were in the living room, and I turned to see if someone was coming in, but no one was there. Tica said, "Your neighbor seems attracted to what's going on." I guess he was sensitive to the energy of channeling. This happened several more times during different channeling sessions—bumps with no one there, and I never found out who it was.

I asked Tica if he was fifth-dimensional, and he responded, "I know the difference, kid." I guess that answered my question. He said we are all here to experience life in all its forms. He explained that he remembers drinking and living it up, but he doesn't define himself by it. It was an experience and now a memory, but he continues to honor that memory. Not all memories are ones we want to honor, but they are a part of us. He also said, "Stand true to what you believe in. Don't let anybody take away what belongs to you."

Tica would rock back and forth in a chair we had for that purpose. I asked him about something I read in a New Age newsletter—that there is a dark star called Merope. I asked, "What role does it play in our planet's evolution and that of the people?" He stopped rocking. He said that dense energies have always played a part in this planet's history and continue to do so today. They are the glue of this dimension. But light energy, growth, and expansion also play a role and will continue as long as there is life. He was always brief in his answers, content to just rock and talk about simple things. It reminded me that there is as much beauty in sharing each other's company as there is in a galaxy full of stars. I only talked to him a few times, but I loved his style and personality.

There was another night, a few days later, when I came home from work. Somé was already home, and I could hear Kitaro's music playing in the bedroom. We often used this music to set the mood for channeling or to relax. As I walked into the room, he was sitting on the bed with his eyes closed. I thought the music was too loud, so I turned it down. Then, from Somé's mouth came a booming, "I am ALL in ALL." The voice was authoritative, exacting, and deep. I thought, "Whoa, this is new, and I have no idea what's happening." He opened his eyes, looked at me, and said, "I see you're listening to one of my spirits." I asked, "Who are you?" "I am everything that ever has been and will be," was the reply.

"Why are you here?" I asked.

"I was summoned," he replied.

Apparently, Somé was asking his own spirits about his purpose and why he was here, and they escalated. It sounded like he had summoned the highest source possible, which was mind-blowing. I tried to make the most of this opportunity and not sound foolish. I asked why we are here. "To gain experience," he answered.

"What keeps us from realizing our full potential?" I asked.

"Fear," was his answer.

"Where does the fear come from?" I was getting desperate.

He simply said, "Man." I could tell he was starting to fade away. After all, he didn't come to talk to me. He closed his eyes and just like that, he was gone. Somé came back and explained that he kept asking deeper questions, and before he knew it, Source was there. Looking back, it wasn't that Spirit couldn't answer; it served some purpose for Somé and maybe for me to share with you. I don't know why, though. I probably asked Spirit a million questions over the years (they call me Mr. Question, among other things). They were kind enough to put up with me, never judging or dismissing me. Somé would also say that sometimes he would ask a question and get no answer. To him, that meant there was no need for an answer at that time. I could ask the same question later and get an answer. It just depended on where we were on our path.

After the frog event in Pebble Beach, Somé asked for protection for both of us. Spirit said that four angels were assigned to us, skilled in understanding third and fourth-dimensional realities. When we leave home, two of them stay, and two go with us. They are seventh-dimensional spirits with a lot of earthly experience. They will be with us for the rest of our lives, and when Somé passes over, they will stay with me.

Back to the San Francisco session.

A Higher Channel

Montaviel said, "Now we come into some uncomfortable times. Why is it uncomfortable? We don't know where we're going, what we're looking for, what we're thinking. We don't know what's real or not real. It's wonderful. It's the best time of your life. You will look back and say, 'Whoa! I didn't know what I had.' Even in all the misery you think you're going through right now, it's an illusion. It's a real illusion, but an illusion, nonetheless. It's part of an ongoing dream. It's real, but it has nothing to do with YOU. Your experience has nothing to do with YOU if you choose to believe that it has nothing to do with you. It's the experience, not you. You are not your experience. Never can be, never will be. It's a hard reality to conceive, but it's a very important one. It's one we have to consider when we make choices.

"Why am I stressing this so much? Because this is what you're asking for. Not in the limited sense of what you're thinking, but this is what you're asking. I'm making it as clear as I can: that that choice is a beautiful choice. It's a wonderful choice. There's nothing wrong with having that choice. But with the choice comes different realities, much different from what you've known. It can't be the same because you're working under a different reality when you have another person with you. It's a whole different reality base. You're not only working on a 16,000-reality base; you have the reality base of 25,000 that this person brings.

"So, then we have many things going on. Talk about mass confusion. One part of us, the emotional part, overwhelms us in the experience. That's the controlling factor we give the experience. It's this tiny part of ourselves in the expansiveness of who we really are. We only want to give credit to one little thing. What about the other parts of you that are crying out to be heard? There are many parts of you crying out to be heard. Yet, we only want to acknowledge one part, the feeling. It's a beautiful thing to have, a wonderful thing to have.

"I wouldn't want it any other way. But until you experience something different to give you a new perspective, you will never feel different about the experience and the face it brings. There's so much more to you. So much more to everyone. You're not any more special than anyone else, and you're all going through the same thing. A lot of people have a much harder time. What you're going through is like this speck on the table compared to what some people are going through.

"In our reality of experience, it's devastating. And it's meant to be. It's meant to be remembered as devastating. That's the importance of the experience. Every experience you have, every feeling you have. If the feeling is good, you say it's a great experience. If the feeling is bad, it's a horrible experience. But you learn much more from the horrible one than from the good one. That brings richness into creating a new reality and a new person.

"Not all of these are good times. Not the precious moments you hold on to. Not as much as it takes away from the feeling you give credit to. The precious moment is wiped away because of the emotion and the vastness of the experience and how we feel the loss. The experience you're trying to create now is about wanting this little piece of you back, and you're willing to cover up the existence of the whole person to let this little piece of you exist. That's what you're asking for. You're asking for one feeling and one feeling only. That's not what you originally asked for. That's why the events took place as they did. You asked, and we delivered. Pick up and go, or however you say it. I have to make light of this because the seriousness you want to place on it is not really there. I know you want..."

Brent said with emotion, "It's serious to me, though."

Montaviel replied, "I know it's serious to you in how you're thinking today. If you want to feel and think this way for the rest of your life, you can. These are not hard choices. Easy. You know what you had, and you can have that forever. But you don't know what's ahead. How could you? Why would you want to choose the unknown? I don't know. But 22 million people do it every day. Yet, 6 billion don't. Why should you be the one to take the risk?

"Let Joe take the risk, and you watch him. If he fails, you won't try it. We put ourselves as the protector of our little selves, watching others and saying, 'They're failing... Oh, they're doing well.'

"What makes us think we know what's going on with others? We only see one part of it, the limited reality. You're experiencing only a small part of yourself, not your wholeness. Now, in the direction you're going today, excluding the possibility," Montaviel turned to Alavan, "which I don't like to say but have to for your sake, excluding the possibility of this other person coming back into your life, are you willing to take the risk for 11 years?"

Brent asked, "11 years?"

Montaviel replied, "Yes, you take the risk of finding your wholeness, and it will take 11 years to find it completely."

Brent asked, "Or I could have Alisal back or take the risk of finding my complete wholeness?"

Montaviel said, "I'm not talking about just one experience. I mean many experiences over time. But to find the complete wholeness of yourself, it's 11 years from today if you take that road. Or you can have 20, 40, 60, or 72.3 years with what you have now. Identical. Nothing changes. Identical. You can have either. I won't say no to you. I can't," Montaviel shook his head.

"That doesn't mean you won't be with anyone else for 11 years. We are talking about finding the complete wholeness of yourself. Alavan and Somé were together for quite a while before they found their wholeness. It took five years from the first day to the day they completed it. Midnight, five years later. That's their wholeness. Not in their reality. Not in yours. They'll never have that reality in their minds. Never. Why? Limited expression, limited form. There are too many limits to comprehending the vastness of what we can believe and see for ourselves. We put limits on everything instead of seeing the vastness of the experience. Somé will never think he's complete because he remembers who he used to be. But the memory is there for protection. It's a tool. It is very important to have. But the limited-form experiences are thought of as memories, making you feel like you're still part of that experience. You're not reliving it. But the effect of the experience is everlasting. Centuries worth. That's what experience is. Once you experience the moment, it becomes embedded within your memory cells.

"Memory. You can never lose it. It's part of your spirit. Memory. So, your choice in what you want to accumulate and how long it takes has no reference to us. It has no meaning to us. You have to place meaning in your reality daily. You have to do that," Montaviel pointed at Brent. "Not us. We can't do that. It's your job," Montaviel chuckled. "Where I work, I could clean this place up in 30 seconds. But that's not part of the experience. Even the useless things we encounter and their usefulness for you are part of your reality, not mine.

"And it's not who you are either. I could walk around saying I am this stick (holding a cigarette), and people would think I'm crazy. See? I am my emotion. I am my feeling. I am my one experience in life.

Alavan said, "It's a good analogy."

Montaviel continued, "I could be all of them. I want to be the stick, the light that makes the stick, the smoke, the smell, the sight, the sound, the feeling, the touch. I want to be it all. I don't want to be just one part of this working reality. That's why it's up to him (gestured toward Brent). I have no control over what I want for him. I am just something up there (pointed to his head) that has all the control and none of the control at the same time."

Alavan said, "Paradox."

Montaviel replied, "Boy, that's a good one. I hold all the cards and none of the cards. It's tricky to conceive a reality based on that. You have it all, and you have nothing."

Montaviel picked up a cigarette, and Brent lit it for him. "This is very, in your terms, enlightening," he nodded slowly. "Maybe 'enlightening' is too expansive for this reality. Let's tone it down. Different. That's a better word... different. How many parts of your mind do you use in one day?"

Brent answered, "I mean, you know, when I drive, I use different parts of my mind than when I'm sitting here or at work."

Montaviel said, "You use parts of your mind and parts of your body that have nothing to do with thought. But if you couldn't do it, it becomes an overwhelming thought. How many times do you blink in three minutes? Sixty-one times. Now, what if you couldn't blink? Suddenly, not blinking becomes a constant thought. Your eyes would dry out, right? How much do you think about how many times you blink? That's how everything really is. Everything works nicely whether you think about it or not. It's your choice to think about it. You choose to think about whether your eyes blink, how many times you swallow, or how much of your mind you use. These things don't interest you because they work automatically. You've put your life on automatic. You don't want to think about it. You just want it to be the way you want it to be because it feels good."

Brent said, frustrated, "But I do have to think about it."

Montaviel replied, "No, you don't. Only in a very limited sense do you have to think about it when it's right in front of you. And what do you think about? You don't think about yourself." He shook his head slowly. "I can count the hours you actually thought about yourself in one year. Hours, we're talking about. And how many hours were you together? Several thousand. But how many hours were you really there for you? Only in the beginning. Then you lost sight because you already decided what you wanted in your life. After making the decision, you saw the reality you were living with and thought, 'If I don't change the way I see it, I lose it.' That's a built-in mechanism. We don't think about it; it happens automatically. Thinking about it would mean changing it, so we can't think about it. Thinking about it would mean it's going to happen even faster."

Brent said, "So, I started thinking about that... about me changing. And that's what started..."

Montaviel interrupted, "Before you moved."

Brent continued, "Before we moved from..." He pointed in a direction, and Montaviel nodded affirmatively.

Montaviel said, "Mmhmm, yeah."

Brent asked, "You mean I started thinking about a positive change for me?"

Montaviel confirmed, "Yes."

Brent said, "And that started the diminishment of..."

Montaviel nodded, "Yes."

Alavan said, "But then you changed because it threatened the relationship."

Montaviel replied, "But that was not our intent. That's not your intent. But that was the choice. We're only fulfilling the choice. What are we supposed to do? We fulfilled the choice by expanding the experience into what you needed. Now, you make another choice along the way, and all it does is delay everything. So, your choices had to come very quickly. You thought, 'I can no longer think of myself. I have to come second.' That was easy, but painful and uncomfortable. I remember the anguish like it was yesterday. In that choice, the hardest choice in your conscious mind was the mystery that there was something better inside you, something different that you were not connected to, that you wanted to be, that was honest, sincere, and heartfelt."

Montaviel snapped his fingers. "Zappo! We all got to work to make it possible. We made it possible for you to fulfill your reality, achieve a goal, and have a third-dimensional reality in another place, which you felt was fulfilling, but it was actually pulling you apart. You have so many different things going on that you can't limit yourself to one. You have a million thoughts at once. So why only one feeling? You should have a million feelings at once. Your feelings should match your thoughts. But we don't do that for a reason."

Alavan said, "A similar thing happened to me. I was with someone, feeling comfortable, thinking we would grow together and do wonderful things. In my reality at the time, I made the same statement to Spirit."

Montaviel replied, "There you go."

Brent said, "You did the same thing?"

Montaviel asked, "But in your conscious mind, did you ever think that would happen?"

Alavan said, "No."

Montaviel continued, "How could it? Impossible. That's the limitation you place on your reality. Not the expansiveness."

Brent asked, "Yes, but was that an honest feeling for you? Was that your reality when you were with her?"

Alavan answered, "Yeah. Because of the many challenges I faced with her, one of the first things Spirit said, Zitron said, was that the probability was we would have a child, the child would channel, and all this stuff. That was music to my ears at the time. In my reality, then, it was 100% true. It was exactly true in my mind." He gestured to Montaviel.

Montaviel said, "Exactly. The sincerity, devotion, honesty, and clarity in how you felt were all there. Strong." Montaviel looked at Brent. "Just as strong as what you're feeling now."

Brent said, "But..."

Montaviel continued, "And he had to let go of that situation in 30 seconds. That was the only choice he had. He was given a choice. He could have had that or something unknown. His choice. Thirty seconds later, he gets up, walks away, and it's over. Zitron was ready if he wasn't because what had to happen was already set (referring to the May 5th event in the ravine)."

Alavan said, "I just had to decide what part of the role I wanted to play, if any."

Montaviel agreed, "It depended on what part of the experience you wanted to play."

Brent said, "I don't see that your experience was the same because you had two people there."

Alavan said, "That part's different, mmhmm."

Brent continued, "And you had Somé. I don't have that. I have nobody."

Alavan asked Montaviel, "How much emotion did I have for Somé in the romantic sense?"

Montaviel replied, "None. Nonexistent. He didn't know what to do. Fear. He had a lot of fear."

Turning to Brent, he said, "When you were with this other person, who else did you have? You had two people in your life, just like he had when he was with Paige. Three people were living in the house with them. His experience and feelings with this one person did not include the others in the house. Your experience with Alisal is one experience. Having two people close to you to share that experience is identical. His experience and what he went through are identical to what you're going through. Nothing different. No more or less. His essence allowed him to experience more than just emotion. He wasn't tied to one part. His essence is different. We see it differently, but what he feels is no less than what you feel. No less, just that we don't see it.

"He was planning a life around one person. Somé was there, planning their life together, trying to keep the couple together. He went beyond what Spirit would have allowed. But we let it happen because Somé needed to learn he can't keep something together that isn't meant to be. But did he try? Yes. Was his emotion real? Yes. Somé cried for 14 days straight, blaming himself for their breakup. You can't imagine the torment he went through. He thought his faith in Spirit was to keep them together. When that didn't work, where was his faith in Spirit? Gone. He said the same things you did, 'I don't need this. I don't want it.' Why? Because it didn't agree with what he wanted. But why should it always agree with what we want? What do we know about what we want? How can you be the sole source of what you want? If you think you are, it's checkout time. Because it's over. There's nothing more to experience. If you want to be the sole coordinator, the sole essence of your experience, you don't need anyone else. There are many out there doing it. You don't need anyone because you're in full control. You know exactly what you want. And no matter what anyone says, you now decide not only which parts of you will participate but who is in control of the universe as well. And we are all one person, the whole universe. We are all of it. And we limit ourselves to one little experience. One. Why do we do this to ourselves when there's a world of information, a world of people to experience? Because as one person, we're all part of them. We're all the same. No different. No greater, no less. Yet we want to control our own little environment, our own safe feeling, because our feelings dictate what's right and wrong. If it feels good, it's real. If it's a thought we're supposed to have, it's real.

"What about all the other things that go on? Are those not real? I see it all as real. Everything is real. Am I going to limit myself to one small part of my feelings and let that control my whole being? I don't think so. I can't. You can. And everybody else in this life form has that ability. I don't anymore. I don't have that ability. I wouldn't want it if I had it. I have no use for that ability because I know I'm there anyway. I have what you have (to Alavan). I have what you have (to Brent). I have it in here. I don't need the face. I have 16 billion faces. I don't need one face. I have them all. I know that doesn't give you the feeling you want because you do want one person to experience this with. And I think you should have it. I know you will have it, and I know the choice you will make. And I know you'll be very happy with that choice. That's all I have to say about that. It's not going to change anything. What I'm trying to change is the way you think about it.

"It's not going to change what will happen. I wouldn't change it if I could. I just want you to know that with your choices, which we already know that a vast array of events happens with every choice. There are choices you make that you cannot even comprehend the consequences of."

Chapter 9: Dimensions

Early on, we had many conversations about higher spirits and fourth-dimensional spirits. Most people think of disembodied spirits as ghosts that wander around. This is true, but those represent a very small fraction of Earth's actual spirit/energy activity. And by that, I mean within and around every one of us.

It was shared that most people have four higher spirits (we met one person who had five). In our case, our higher spirits were once in form, but not usually on Earth. They were in form on planets that have since become stars. For us, those stars are Polaris and Tekstar. We all know Polaris, the North Star. I haven't found any references to Tekstar in my research, but Spirit refers to it as the pink star, representing emotion. Polaris is the blue star and represents thought. For Somé, most of his spirits are from Tekstar, so he first processes everything through his emotional body. Most of my spirits are from Polaris, so while I have a great deal of emotion as well, I process everything through my mental body first. I tend to be analytical while Somé needs to feel what he's doing first. We are both a mix of pink and blue.

I recall a gold star and a purple star as well, but never received names for them. These folks who have higher spirits from these stars have physical expressions and process their experiences mostly through their physical bodies.

A Higher Channel

Just for reference, the dimensional levels of fifth-dimensional spirits are fifth, seventh, tenth, and fourteenth. People usually connect with one of their four higher spirits. Somé connected most with Zitron, his seventh-dimensional spirit. I connect with Alava, my fourteenth. The dimensional number indicates the degree of separation from the third/fourth dimension. Technically, the higher the number, the more "big picture" they are. Somé channeled very few fourteenth-dimensional spirits because they are further removed from the day-to-day stuff on Earth. Most of the spirits that Somé channeled were either seventh or tenth-dimensional. Those spirits have a frame of reference that is relatable.

We return to the San Francisco channeling session.

Montaviel continued, "When you put something in your mouth, you think it's all automatic. Everything will go down fine, and it will come out fine. But suddenly, there's a consequence to that choice. You thought, 'Oh, I never even considered I'd feel this way from eating this.' That's the consequence of the choice.

"So, I don't care what your thoughts and choices are; there are reactions to everything. And I see them all as part of the learning experience, all of it. You don't place much emotion on putting something in your mouth and getting indigestion, but how much less is that experience than this? Identical. It's only in your mind that you want to place one as being more powerful than the other. It can't be and never will be.

"The experience and the feeling you have when looking at a sunset by yourself is more enlightening to your wholeness than being with 16 million people. There is more richness in that than what many people can give you. But six hundred people in this city alone are waiting for the chance to knock at your door. Six hundred. And those you have a connection to, twenty-two."

Brent asked, "That I know?"

Montaviel replied, "You see them off and on quite frequently, and the energetic connection is strong, just like with Alisal. Nine of them are four times stronger, and two are way out there. But these eyes (points to his eyes) make you look away when they come by. That's the sad part about the limits we place on our own realities. You look the other way. It doesn't feel right, so you ignore it. This tiny speck (points at a speck on the table) seems to know more than the universe. This speck gets all the credit. The universe gets nothing."

Montaviel continued, "And so you look the other way. Nine people you are in constant communication with can energetically give you more in two minutes than this other person could. There's so much out there that we don't allow ourselves to do."

Brent asked, "But why? If they're there and I know them, why don't I recognize them? Why doesn't anybody say anything to me?"

Montaviel said, "They have. But you take someone else's word and perceive things differently. You think they're just joking or trying to make you feel good. They have more sincerity and honesty in their hearts for you than most people can dream of. Yet you look the other way instead of embracing that acknowledgment and seeing what your heart can feel instead of what your eyes see. Our eyes become limited with blinders, and we diminish the experience. It's part of who these limited bodies are. They keep everything controlled and easy. But when you erase that and say, 'I'm ready, let it go,' you'll see the difference. Talk to Alavan and Somé about their experience in this form. Ask them how fast you have to move in your thoughts. If you want to go at their pace, you can. It will probably give you two hours of sleep a week."

Alavan laughed, "Maybe not that bad. It was pretty rough in the beginning, though."

Montaviel said, "It's seven hours, exactly seven hours a week on average, that they slept for the first seven months because they were willing to take that risk. As painful and unrealistic as it seemed, they did it. Was it painful? Oh, yeah. Did they want to quit? Oh, yeah. Hundreds of times. But what drove them was knowing what they had. They thought, 'I have all this experience. This is wonderful.' Not quite the terms they used then," he added with laughter and agreement. "But the richness of their past experience, which they didn't even understand fully, made them say, 'I gained all I can gain from this. Now let me go with the wind.'

"And that's how fast it went. They went with the wind, and it came at such a pace that it was overwhelming. At times, they did have to slow down and stop. And when they said slow down, Spirit said fine. All right, slow down. No more. It stopped just as quickly. So, the thought, feeling, the desire, the honesty of your feeling can happen whenever you want it to.

"Anything can happen. The possibilities for you to enhance the universe are there. Now we're just talking about probabilities because we're looking at your choices. Somé talks so much about your probabilities in choices because that's where it lies, and that's up to everybody. We have nothing to say about your choice. Nothing. We don't want to. Don't need it."

Montaviel retrieved a cigarette out and said that Somé likes his cigarettes.

Brent said, "Yes, he does like his cigarettes. I didn't smoke until I got with the three of them." He laughed.

Montaviel said, "We bring out the best in everyone." Everyone laughed. "In more ways than one. We can look at it lightly because that's how we want to see it. But bringing out the best in everyone comes from a reality about helping someone else. There's a feeling you get, and you know what that feeling is like. The experience of doing something for someone else not only enhances you, but you also see it bringing out the best in them. It can be anything, like making something for someone or offering a gift. Like what you did for them (Brent making a domestic partnership cake for Alavan and Somé) a week ago last Monday. Just that one small act, in all the anticipation of new realities you're going through, affected 117 people, not just you. One act of making a cake. Unbelievable. Just by one thing. So don't limit your mind to thinking you're doing this for one person. This one person holds the key to the universe just like you do. You don't do it just for one. You do it for everyone. You're not becoming whole just for yourself. You're doing it for everybody. That's the expansiveness of what spirituality holds in all of us. It's not just us. It's everybody."

Brent said, "Why can't...the one thing I liked was that Somé, Alavan, Alisal, and I were a group."

Montaviel replied, "Still are."

Brent continued, "But... I want us to be... I know we're still a group. I know we can go out together. You know, it just..."

Montaviel said, "What diminishes the experience? The way you look at it. But what is actually in the experience of the four of you going out? There is more in the experience today than there was three months ago. A lot more. Maybe not in the way you think. Maybe not in the way they think. But there is more wholeness in the experience of the four of you today than there could have ever been before. The feeling may not be there for it."

Brent said, "I know..."

Montaviel continued, "But see, the feeling is not you. That's the whole point."

Brent said, "The feeling is me, though, you know, wanting that comfort with Alisal."

Montaviel said, "The feeling is a mechanism…"

Brent interrupted, "Being with Somé and Alavan now, seeing their companionship with the two of us as acquaintances, it just doesn't work. It doesn't work for me. That's not wholeness to me. Sure, I can become more whole. I don't feel comfortable with the idea of bringing in another person or people. That doesn't seem whole to me."

Montaviel asked, "So, what do you want to do?"

Brent said, "It just seems like... It seems like I fail all the way around..." Brent sobbed. "I know that by wanting Alisal back so badly, it seems like I failed. I fail Somé and Alavan. I fail the whole desire for wholeness. But by making another choice not to be with him, it seems like I fail that way too because I don't know."

Montaviel asked, "Can you conceive the possibility that it's impossible to fail at anything? I'll tell you why you can't conceive that. You don't want to. You want to see things as black and white, right and wrong, good and evil. That's the way you think. That's the way you want to think.

"Is there anything wrong with it? No. It's a limited expression. It's a limited view of the expansiveness of what the universe offers. It's just a very limited way to look at it. Can we look at it that way and be happy? Oh, yes. Definitely. That's also your choice. You can have what you consider to be everything, and in having everything, do you still have anything? You tell me, what do you have?"

Brent said, "I have that feeling of comfort."

Montaviel asked, "Okay. For how long?"

Brent stammered, "The only thing I can think of is I want that comfort for the rest of my life. For the rest of my existence on this planet."

Montaviel said, "So, you're willing to go to any extreme, to any cost, to achieve that feeling? And it's not wrong to say yes. I know you want to say yes."

Brent replied, "I know I want to say yes. You know better than I do."

Montaviel said, "Yes, exactly. There's nothing wrong with that. There's nothing wrong with what you want. Nothing wrong. There's nothing right about it, either. It's just the way it is. There's no right or wrong, no black, no white. It's all an extension of one thing. You can't determine right and wrong because you only work on a limited reality. If you want the reality you're working on to determine how you want to live, you have that choice. You can see him as good and everything else as wrong. Or you can say, 'That's just what they do, but this is what I want.'

You become enclosed within your own little box, your own little world, your own limited expression. That's all you have. Nothing wrong with it. There's nothing wrong with that choice and nothing wrong with another choice. The only difference is the way you look at it."

Chapter 10: Energy Portals

As Somé began to learn how energy and spirits moved, he was drawn to the activity in a local bar in Monterey. We would go there on weekends, and what he discovered was fascinating. He said that when someone is interested in someone else, actual spirits and energy are "projected" toward that person. Depending on the willingness or openness of the person receiving the spirits, they are either accepted or rejected. Sometimes the two people ended up talking and leaving together, but usually, it was just energy flying around being ignored or absorbed little by little. Sometimes people were interested in my brother or me, and Somé would block the attempted transfer of energy and try to encourage that person to move along. Most of the time, it worked, but sometimes it didn't. The level of inebriation typically played a huge role in how receptive they were to suggestions. The drunker they were, the less they "listened." There was a big mirror behind the bar, and Somé said that spirits could reflect off that and even move through the mirror.

Somé found that he could help people find moments of grace by guiding the fourth-dimensional spirits that supported them into the light, or fifth dimension. The stronger the reality, the more reluctant the spirits might be. But eventually, they would go. This only worked as long as someone could keep their mind in that state of grace. Typically, it doesn't take long for limited identities and old thought patterns to re-emerge and need energetic support. So, we tend to quickly gravitate back to old realities, even if our mind is completely clear of interference. There are plenty of spirits to help as well. We just need to see them as energy because that's what they are.

Somé set up light portals in every physical location he visited. Bars were the first, due to their heavy activity, followed by restaurants, hotels, and any place we traveled. He did this by touching the door frame and setting up the portal as he walked in. The light portals would attract any fourth-dimensional spirit ready to move to the fifth dimension. The spirits might not know what is happening, but it helps to "lighten the load" overall on the planet. In 1990, the total number of spirits transferred through these portals was around 40,000. The energy of the portals also intensifies over time. By 2014, the total was around 980,000; by 2016, it was over 2 billion. He had set up 604 portals all over the U.S., with some in Europe and New Zealand by 2016.

We asked if there were others like Somé on the planet. The answer was twelve, including Somé, in 2016. Two more were added in 2017. By late 2016, this team had moved 16 billion spirits to the fifth dimension. It is part of the overall work being done on this planet.

Somé wrote down some of his learnings while working with people. Below is an entry from August 1995:

August 1995

> One of the most interesting things I can do is watch people and their reactions and listen to them talk. You can learn a lot from this. I've noticed that the energy exchanged between two people is played out differently for each person. The only experience I have with this is the experience that Alavan and I had in the past. Our exchange of energy was equal, making the experience more balanced. We learned to meet each other's needs more easily, making it a learning experience for both of us. I could learn from him, and he could learn from me. It wasn't easy; it was the hardest lesson we had to learn.
>
> In watching Brent and Alisal, I am reminded of the experience Alavan and I had together. Brent and I are similar in how we display our feelings. But now, I see that even though it looked the same, it really isn't. Each person experiences life differently. I've noticed that Brent is taking on more energy from Alisal. This makes their experience different from mine and Alavan's. The way Brent reacts to things now is nothing like he would have in the past. This is good in one sense, but I feel it might make the process

longer than it has to be. But who's to say this isn't the best way for them? It's just different from what I expected.

I find it difficult for people to understand the concept of transpersonal relationships. I hope that by watching them and remembering the process Alavan and I went through, I can better understand the problems others are having. Each day, I feel closer to this understanding.

Aug. 4, 1995

I've learned a lot from talking to different people and hearing what they say. I've found that just because they have thought about doing something, it doesn't mean it will happen. There is a natural process in how energy works through thought. Having the thought is just the first step. Most people think that just having the thought means everything will work out. It doesn't. The saying "it's the thought that counts" is not really correct. People say this to get themselves off the hook or justify someone else's actions. What I have found works more correctly with the universe is that once you have the thought, you need to express it in words and then in action. If your action doesn't represent your word and thought, it moves into the universe without direction. This is one of the great misconceptions we have in the Western world. I would rather see positive action from people, even if it comes from a misguided thought. It is much easier to correct the thought than the action. Once the action moves into the universe, it makes a statement about you.

Aug. 10, 1995

It seems to me that it doesn't really matter how I say things to people or how intensely I say them. How they perceive it has more to do with them than with what I say. Recently, I've watched people I've been doing a lot of energy work with. I think I could have done much less energy work and got the same results. I know this is true because, on many occasions, I have deliberately done just that. So now I have decided to do very little energy work with people. It really takes a lot out of me when I do this. I can feel a drastic energy change in myself. If it's not going to make a difference in the intensity I work with, I will choose to talk to them without doing the energy work. What surprises me is to watch people take on opposite energy changes from their partners. Even with these opposite energy changes, the dominant energy stays the same. It may not look like it from a third-dimensional perspective, but I feel it remains true.

For example, a person who always shows a lot of compassion for another person slowly starts to change. He starts to forget what he has done in the past and takes on the energy of his partner. Someone who always remembers dates, appointments, and events suddenly forgets he even mentioned them. The dominant person appears to have changed to many other people, including his partner. This is where the dominant person takes charge in every situation, even without their partner knowing. This is why people in relationships don't really change. They think they are changing, but it is only in their own minds. If anyone really wants to change, they have to be willing to give up everything that represents their old self. They say they want this, but from what I have seen, it doesn't happen. They seem to pick and choose what they want in their lives. They always pick and choose what they think is different, but in reality, it's the same. To be someone different is one of the hardest reality changes you will ever make. To be willing to give up oneself is not real in anyone's mind. The reality is that you don't give up anything; you gain the most important reality in your life—yourself and your Spirit.

Aug. 12, 1995

Why is change so hard for people? Why does giving up old realities feel like death? Even the desire to change is not enough. It has to go beyond just wanting to change.

Something in your life has to show you that the way you've lived is not what you really want. I've found that every person has an energy level representing that change. Your thoughts might be telling you it's time to change only because it's what everyone around you is doing. This doesn't mean it's time for you. How do you know if this energy is at the right level for you? I believe everyone knows; they're just unfamiliar with the signs Spirit gives them. The only way to know if it's right for you is to listen to your own Spirit. They are the only ones that truly know you. None of us really know at any given time what is right for us. We all want to believe that we have control over our own lives. But believing this shows how this reality has messed us up. The world wouldn't be in its current state if we knew what we were doing.

Aug. 14, 1995

In watching and learning from people as they go through these changes, I have used most of my past experiences to relate to them. It has helped quite a bit, but it doesn't seem to make a difference in many cases. People have to experience these changes themselves in reality. Even hearing what I went through doesn't seem to connect very well. Everyone has their own way to go through their process. I always hope that, in some small way, there is something I can say or do to make the energy change in them so they can start to see a new reality. I know I'm not in charge of making this happen—their own spirit is. Only your own spirit can truly get this across to you. The only thing I can do is make the energy more accessible for you to understand. Here are several points each person can look for in themselves:

Accept that there are different ways to look at each situation.

Accept that you have a higher spirit (angel, guide, or any higher source other than yourself).

Accept the possibility that the information you receive from your higher spirit will help you apply new realities to yourself.

By accepting these first three new realities, you can create a new reality. (A reality is a thought, word, or action that becomes real for you.) Always remember that when creating a new reality, you never lose your true self.

August 23, 1995

So many things have happened in the last few days, and my mind has been going in all different directions. I know I'm following my spirit when I help others, but the results are where I struggle. I can't seem to stop even when I know the person I'm talking to isn't understanding me. I realize it's not my place to worry about these things, but it still affects me. I put too much energy into issues when I already know the outcome. I'm taking these issues too personally. Spirit always reminds me that I can't change anything. As I prepare for the reopening of the New Life Center, these issues are on my mind. I thought I had this under control, but after last night, I see I don't. Before starting this session today, I had a long talk with Spirit. I need to control my personal feelings and thoughts. With Spirit's help, I know I can do this. Every time I act or think, Spirit guides me on how to feel. I know this feeling well, but I often overlook it. There should be no difference in working with someone I know versus someone I don't. Spirit has told me that having personal issues with someone only drains my energy, which I don't want. This past month, I've been trying to maintain an even energy level. I thought I was doing well until I talked to Spirit today. I need to stay focused on what I do. With this in mind, I think about how personally I've treated Brent and Alisal. I don't want to be hard on them, but Spirit has told me that making things easy isn't helpful. From now on, I need to be straightforward. I know Brent won't have a problem with this, but Alisal might. It already seems like I'm always picking on him. I've tried to make it as easy as possible, but I realize now that I won't be doing as much as I have in the past. I need to be honest with myself and with him. I need to step back. In all other areas of my life, everything is going great. I feel better now than ever before. I credit Alavan and Spirit for giving me an incredible life.

August 25, 1995

Brent and Alisal came over last night, and for the first time, I kept my mouth shut. I could have said many things, but I didn't. I'm very happy with myself. I felt the emotion rise, but I didn't lose any energy. It's not that hard to just listen without responding. At the end of the night, I felt much better. I must admit there was a small part of me that wanted to say something. Where I would have spoken in the past, I now feel a sense of calm. I know now that it's not hard to do. Taking a non-personal approach to every situation will be much easier for me. I do it with everyone else, so now I have to do it with those closest to me. I can almost feel Spirit patting me on the back. They don't, but it feels like they do when I follow my spirit. Following my spirit is becoming automatic; I don't even have to think about it. It's getting harder to know when I am, but I can tell immediately when

I'm not. This makes me think about the learning process. I've always said it's impossible to know where you're going, but you always know where you've been. It's also impossible to know what you really want in life, but you always know what you don't want. Your past experiences are the only indicators of what you don't need to participate in. (Somé, 1995)

Back to the San Francisco session.

Montaviel spoke to Brent: "It's not that I don't agree with you. I do, but only from one part of your reality. Just one part. I can see it, feel it, taste it. I can sense the whole essence of that experience in one reality. I know you, and I know the reality shifts you put upon yourself, and you do it frequently for a reason. Yes, this person could be back in your life tomorrow, but your reality won't allow it.

"It can happen, and you can struggle with it, fight it. You know what it's like. You can go through it again. He can leave again and come back again. We can keep this up as long as you want. We have nothing else better to do. You can do that, hoping his reality will change to match yours. But there's more risk in *that* than walking into the unknown.

"The risk is much higher. It's a thousand times greater. Why? Look at your experience. Don't let it fool you. Your experience is a picture of yourself. Don't expect the experience to be any different unless you're different. If you keep the same mindset, you'll have the same experience again, just at a different time. That's how most people live. It's widely accepted. But honestly, knowing you as I do, and boy, do I know you, you won't settle for that. You can't. There's a mechanism within you that gets triggered by this type of experience, revealing something different about yourself than what you're used to. These mechanisms drive you to act in ways that ultimately harm your relationship, causing it to end.

Alavan interjected, "Alisal has the same mechanism. How do you think it all came about the first time?

Montaviel responded, "That's how. That's the only way it was possible. Now, how many times do you want to experience the same thing? A few? If you said 20, we can do 20.

"I don't want to experience that...," Brent said.

"We'll get to 20 really quickly because I know what's pressing in your mind," Montaviel replied. "It's the fight. You're going to fight to save your soul before you save anything else. That comes first with you. Whether you want to acknowledge it consciously or not, you are going to fight to save your soul. That takes precedence over anyone else. Yet you're letting a small part of you say, 'No, no, no, no, no.' So, you return to the same experience, doing the same thing even with someone else. The same thing. Because you want it the same, but the essence of your soul won't let you. It's saying, 'No, no, no, no. We know what it's like. We've done it. See ya!' And then you move on. That's what experience is about. But don't dismiss the emotions and feelings of the experience. You need them. You need them more than air."

Chapter 11: Are Those Stars?

A couple of months after the event in May, we moved to Carmel Valley and rented a house with my brother, Alisal, who worked nearby at the Carmel Valley Lodge. This house had decks that provided a nice view of the valley and a clear view of the night sky because there was little ambient light. The next few months would offer more growth opportunities for Somé as he continued to hone his craft and explore its possibilities. We also learned some things that blew our minds.

One night after we moved into the house, around August 5th, 1990, Somé and I were out on the deck off the main bedroom, looking at the stars. The air was crisp and clear, and the view was spectacular. However, one star caught my attention. It wasn't bigger or brighter, but it seemed to be blinking different colors. I looked at other stars to verify they weren't blinking. They weren't. But this star was clearly blinking different colors and shone brighter than the others. I thought it might be a plane and waited for it to move, but it didn't. I figured it must be closer, which might explain the flashing colors.

I asked Somé if he could sense anything, and I wasn't prepared for his answer. He said they were ships performing energy work as part of the energetic expansion. Apparently, they position themselves in front of stars as a sort of cloaking mechanism. Somé was talking back and forth with his spirit and said he was going to lie down and communicate with the ones on the ship. I grabbed a pen and a pad of paper to document it all.

Somé said the ship was a light vessel from the 4th/5th dimension. He communicated with Tricus from the 7th dimension, who is a "receiver" or communicator. Before each greeting, they say, "Oombasha," which is a greeting and homage in the language from Polaris. Somé's spirits use this language, so they speak it as well. The leader introduced himself/herself as Pompei. Somé said that as they greeted him, their arms were outstretched with palms facing up.

Pompei explained that they were a high-energy light ship performing work in this area, assisting walk-ins and other energetic expansion efforts. The introduction continued. I will spell the names as phonetically as possible: Tomal, Cancoso (ship captain and communicator), Saposei, Meihei, Croton, Mexta, Aresto, Neekey, Omeisei, Cruton, Titus, Rekstan, Teileimeishei, Tomei, Meishei, Sandopu, Elici, Seimei, and Creesei – 21 in all but I missed a couple of the names. Their bodies aren't like what we typically understand beings in ships to be, but there are some similarities. Somé said their bodies are like ours, just more transparent, with larger heads and ears and vocal cords. Since he had done a lot of energy work with people, I asked how far their vibrational energies radiated. He reported the following:

Physical – 18 inches from the body

Mental – 3 feet

Emotional – 6 inches

Spiritual – 8 feet

He also said that there are smaller ships as well. This ship measured 85 feet in length, 62 feet wide, and 16 feet high. They are gathering data from dolphins. They mentioned that a transition team from the 7th system would be coming soon. There would be five walk-ins within the next two years, the first in six months.

Six months later, on February 5th, 1991, they came back. We had just sat down for dinner when Some received a thought from Pompei that they were back. We jumped up and went outside on the deck. We saw the ships in the sky where stars would normally be, glowing brightly.

Pompei was explaining to a group of higher spirits about walk-ins (not complete walk-ins but more of a conscious process) that Quombei, a high-energy lightship, would be doing energy work in this area. There would be 65 walk-ins in various forms. Eight would be in adult form, and seventeen would be in "first-phase" form. He didn't mention what forms the others would take. The second wave team was at work preparing the way to awaken the walk-ins to know their rightful place. However, it will take a full 20 years for the walk-ins to fully understand their place. We will know who they are and will assist in their awakening. They also said very kind words about Somé and me and the work we were doing, reaching thousands of people.

He said that everything is time-related, and the job has just begun. Our own efforts would be intensified 1000 times so that all who "have to know will know."

Pompei then spoke to Somé's 10-dimensional higher spirit, Botra: "You of the first system (Polaris) are being joined by the second, third, fourth, fifth, sixth, and seventh systems at work at this time. Each performing their own magnificent light work upon this planet." He said that we should be ready. This is the most important factor in any time-related sequence. All seven systems are working, each with their own purposeful light work. Each system communicates with us through a different part of our body. By keeping our forms ready, all seven can work effectively. Physical and mental changes will happen rapidly. The seven systems have been here for the past six weeks. Before that, there were only three.

That night was the last we heard from them. We also learned that they perform light work all over the planet and are still working to this day.

In 2007, I asked Botra if there were other systems with ships. He said that out of the 17 systems with life forms, 11 of them have ships. I then asked if they could see each other. He answered, "Only six."

It was also around this time that Somé and I were in a mall parking lot, and he asked me if I could change my name, what would I pick? I thought for a second and told him that I liked the name Alavan. He smiled and said that my highest spirit's name was actually Alava which meant "communication with love". I kept the "n" on the end and use that name to this day.

Back to the San Francisco session.

Alavan chuckled, "This form is pretty beat up. You have to admit it."

Montaviel replied, "It is. Well, if I don't behave, then I can't come back." Alavan and Brent laughed.

Montaviel continued, "I have to stand up."

Brent said, "Yeah, okay. I'm just going to stand right here for support. I may be drawing this on too long. I'm sorry." Montaviel sat back down.

Montaviel responded, "It's my choice how long it goes on. It's one choice I'm making right now to keep going."

Alavan said, "You can stand up for a while if you want. Does he want to stand up?"

Montaviel replied, "I did. He did. We did. Like I said, the amount of time that I'm here has no bearing on anything. It's just to show that all choices are perfect choices, perfect, and all realities that go with those choices are perfect. But it's what the essence of your soul is telling you to do. I have no control. I can't change your essence. Wouldn't want to."

Alavan asked, "Would you say that the nature of everybody's essence is to unfold?"

Montaviel replied, "No. That's a generalization when you say 'everybody'."

Alavan asked, "Is it the nature of us to just keep on going, keep learning, just keep going?"

Montaviel answered, "It's not the essence. Those are built-in, automatic mechanisms that cause you to do things you have no control over. Those aren't choices. Those aren't reality busters. Even in your fight not to move on, you move on. Nothing stays the same. Can't step in the same river twice. Great quote."

Brent mentioned, "Yeah, Alice Walker. That's her new book: The Same River Twice: Honoring the Difficult."

Montaviel responded, "Well, it's people like her and her experiences that unfold into marvelous writings. Marvelous writings. Thomas Paine, a writer from England, is another example. His way of thinking or feeling is unbelievable. Thomas Paine is probably one of the few little-known people who hold the key. Somé holds the key. Thomas Paine holds the key. There are many people who hold that key, but it's not being turned often. But the few times they do, the advantage is tremendous for those who listen and read what these people say. They don't have to be like Jesus was. We don't need people like that now. It doesn't serve any purpose anymore. Two thousand years ago, it served a great purpose. Today, no. We need to work with a reality we all understand. We listen to people who were tremendously abused and people with rich experiences, and it's that richness of experience that shows us the possibility of what can happen. These are the people that hold keys. The keys unlock the presence of the universe."

Montaviel continued, "It is unlimited. But these people only open little, tiny doors. They are capable of opening tremendous doors, but the fear of non-acceptance stops the door from being fully opened."

Alavan asked, "People who read this?"

Montaviel replied, "By people who read this and for people who experience what you, Somé, or anyone else says that holds any information. It's handled in such a way as to prove to everyone else that we want to remain limited. We don't want to have an expanded universal mind. See? We have millions of thoughts. There's only one thought. One. Yet it comes from millions of people and it's one thought. But that one thought is split into a million fragments. That's how we operate, think, and experience things. The limits that we, by our own choice, place upon ourselves to experience only what we want to be comfortable with. He makes me comfortable." Montaviel nods toward Brent.

Brent admitted, "I admit that. I admit that."

A Higher Channel

Montaviel responded, "What's wrong with that? He makes you comfortable. It's a great feeling to have. Somé and Alavan, at this point, are very comfortable. So what do we have to do to make his essence and what he's doing uncomfortable? Well, we place you here; we place Alisal here. We place 26 other people who are in constant communication with him. There's his uncomfortableness. It's eating away at his mind."

Alavan asked, "Oh, Some?"

Montaviel nodded, "Mmhmm. So, if you look at him as being comfortable and relaxed, no."

Brent said, "Well, no, I know. I know he's not. I mean, I'm a great..."

Montaviel continued, "But the relationship part of what they have has stabilized to a point where there's no longer any discussion about the uncomfortableness of that. But being who we are in these limited forms, uncomfortableness has to come from somewhere. It has to."

Alavan said, "So, avoiding it is kind of useless, huh?"

Montaviel replied, "You can't avoid it. You can't learn without it. It's impossible. That's the third time I've said it." Alavan and Brent laughed.

Brent asked, "By choosing to go back with Alisal and have him back in my life, am I also making the choice that he's going to constantly be leaving me over and over?"

Montaviel responded, "That's the chance you take."

Brent said, "And then I have to make the choice to have him back again and then out again and back again?"

Montaviel replied, "The possibility is there, and you know what the experience holds. So why would you think it would be any different? It can be. It can't be. It is. It isn't. What are you willing to settle for? His presence there? Is that the only thing life has to offer you, just his presence?"

Brent hesitated, "No, because…"

Montaviel continued, "That's what you want to believe, though. You want us to believe that that is the key. That is your key to happiness. Your only key. The only part of your existence comes from this one person. Yet, what did this one person offer you in exchange for what you were willing to give?"

Brent replied, "He offered me some knowledge in his limited ways."

Montaviel responded, "Okay."

Brent continued, "Okay. He offered me companionship."

Montaviel replied, "Okay."

Brent said, "Okay. Yes, he offered me pain."

Montaviel responded, "Yes."

Brent continued, "Okay. But he offered me a joy that I've never felt before in my life."

Montaviel replied, "Okay."

Brent admitted, "I'm just going around in circles."

Montaviel explained, "The only reason why you're going around in circles is because you think there is a devastating effect to a choice. There is no devastating effect to any choice. Every choice is a great choice."

Brent said, frustrated, "I know. You're saying every choice is right, but then the choice that I make..."

Montaviel said, "That was right, too. The choice to have him back is right. The choice to have him leave is right. The choice to do something else is right."

Alavan added, "He's just trying to give you an idea of what's involved."

Brent replied, "I know."

Montaviel continued, "It's part of the essence of the experience. What more can you expect? You can't expect somebody to give you more than they are capable of giving. How can you expect that? It's unrealistic to expect somebody to give you more than you've already seen. He gave you all he knew. Can he learn to give more? Oh, sure. He can learn to do that. But now we face his choices. Is he willing to learn?"

Brent said, "See? And that's what I was saying earlier. I meant taking away, you know, taking away his choice."

Montaviel responded, "No, you can't. You can never give to or take away from anyone else's experience. Impossible. The fourth time I've said it. Can't do it. Won't happen. And that's the frustrating part because you think that that experience is it. You put so much of yourself into it, and you think you're doing it for them. No, no, no."

Brent replied, "He wants, he wants, Somé has told me he wants the same thing that I want deep down."

Alavan interjected, "Deep down, yes. So does every human being on the planet."

Montaviel added, "You know what else he wants? He wants love, companionship, everything that you want."

Brent sighed and said, "I know."

Montaviel continued, "Except for one thing. A different face. Why? Why does he have to have a different face? It's because he can't find it here himself." Montaviel pointed to his chest. "Somé said a very powerful thing to him. And it'll ring true from now until the day you're all no longer here. The whole point is that we don't care if you're a man or woman, dog or cat, or with no one. We don't care. You can be with anybody in the world. But if you can't be with the one in here, you're with no one." Montaviel gestured toward his heart. "So, it doesn't matter how much you desire and want this person. If you don't have it in here, you can never have it in someone else.

He can never give you anything you can't give yourself. Impossible. Never happen."

Brent asked, "But am I not giving it to myself either?"

Montaviel replied, "No. You won't even come close to giving it back to yourself."

Brent asked, "So, I can't give it to him?"

Montaviel answered, "No. Impossible." He continued as Brent began to weep. "But that's the nature of everything, you see. If you have it here, it belongs to you. It does not belong to anyone else. It belongs to you. But you have to have it here. And when you have it here, you could care less."

Brent said, "What face it has…"

Montaviel continued, "It makes no difference because I have it right here. I hold the universe in my own heart. The essence of my soul is the universe. I don't care whose face is there. However, there are personal preferences in what we'd like to see."

Brent said, "Sure, I have preferences. I'm a physical being. I have preferences."

Montaviel replied, "We all do."

Chapter 12: Healing Energy and Helping Others

Somé learned that he could move energy through his hands and affect the physical body. He started practicing on himself by focusing healing energy on some nodes on his finger joints just before the tips. He was told they developed because of his years in farming and handling cold produce boxes. He had two nodes as big as marbles. They caused him pain whenever he picked up anything that touched them. He began rubbing them and directing energy through them to break them up and send healing thoughts and colors. White was for breaking them up, and yellow and green for healing.

It only took a few weeks for them to completely disappear. It was amazing.

He also worked with a couple of people from the store where we worked. James had severe back pain and came over a few times for sessions where Somé would redirect energy while also sensing the source of the pain. Sometimes, it was due to unconscious issues, and other times it was purely physical. I remember James saying he felt like he was back in high school and that his outlook was completely changed by this work. He said he felt "invincible." However, in most cases, the results were short-lived, and the symptoms often returned as people tended to go back to old thought patterns and behaviors that caused the issue in the first place. This was a hard lesson for Somé to learn because he put everything he had into trying to help people. He wanted so much for them to feel better permanently, but, like many things in life, it's just not that simple.

Our realities are supported by energy in the form of 4th-dimensional spirits. Somé would explain that removing the "extra" spirits and sending them to the light gave the person clarity and a fresh start. It gave them an opportunity to understand that they can feel different than they do right now—that it's possible to experience life with a sense of grace. It just takes time.

We set up a non-profit organization called the New Life Center, where Somé provided healing services, energy work, and channeled informational sessions. I was there to support the sessions, provide clarity when needed, and, as he would say, keep the energy moving. Everything was free of charge, but donations were accepted. We saw about 30 or so folks over the short time that we ran the New Life Center. We ran ads in the local newspaper about subjects like repressed energy, childhood trauma, and other impactful experiences that led to people not being able to express themselves. Somé could feel stuck energies in people and could also get information on what led to that repression. It was either outright abuse or abandonment. Somé would often get very emotional as he was diving into their past. He couldn't help but feel what the past events created in their reality and what they felt at the time. Spirit always said that the reason for his own abuse was to be able to feel compassion for others.

He worked with one woman, Lacy, who was abused as a child. As he felt her past, he ended up in tears, only to wipe his eyes, raise his head, and share what he had learned and what energy clearing he performed for her. He explained that trauma is very impactful and leaves deep scars—physically, emotionally, and energetically. Healing takes time, but she needed to know that she was beautiful, amazing, and deserved the very best. Nothing that happened to her was her fault. He could tell that she predominantly carried the energy of her mother. We typically carry the energy of one of our parents regardless of whether they raised us. These patterns of experience repeat themselves over lifetimes as we reincarnate with the same players, yet in different roles over lifetimes, but always with a new perspective. Lacy's life had just begun, in a sense. She had rays of sunshine ahead of her. Although the path to healing is never easy, the journey is worth the effort because of who we become as a result.

Another person who came to us was Roger. What was interesting about Roger was that when Somé was feeling Roger's energy and communicating with his higher spirits to get information, Somé found out that Roger had five higher spirits. Normally, everyone has four, so this was different from what we thought was the norm. No specific answer was given as to why, but Somé shared this information with Roger and said that it added to the fabric of who he was. Roger was super creative, a dancer and an artist. If I recall correctly, his spirits were from four different stars in total, which represents a wider range of energetic makeup. Typically, our spirits represent two stars, on average. Roger was unique and a beautiful spirit himself.

I remember asking Spirit how Somé, being completely unfamiliar with and uninterested in any of this stuff, would be chosen to participate in such a huge way. They said that it isn't as new to him as you would think. He was a Tibetan monk in a past life, so many of these concepts aren't new to him at all. In fact, they come naturally.

Back to the San Francisco session.

Brent said, "What's wrong with the person I want to be with?" He looked away, frustrated.

Montaviel replied sarcastically, "Oh, we can change his mind really quick."

Alavan added, "Oh yeah, we already know he'll do that". He referred to Alisal.

Montaviel continued, "And we can make him believe that this is the choice that has to be made. See, he is so easy to work with. He's so easy to manipulate. And is that bad? No, it's not bad because we manipulate everything we do. We manipulate every thought. We manipulate every part of our being, and why? It's the nature of the beast. Manipulation, manipulation, the illusion of control. Why do we do it? That's who we are. With everything we give birth to, we kill. It's the way we are. So, we can put a lot of emotion and a lot of energy into anything we want. It doesn't change it."

Alavan said, "So if we have the universe in our soul, what we end up doing is trying to find it in other people or other experiences or other things. And then, finally, we just realize it's not there; it's here. We just finally realize that?"

Montaviel replied, "It's always been there, except we have to have a visual in front of us to say to ourselves, 'Oh, look what I have. I am now happy.' But when this person leaves, my happiness goes too. So, what gave you the right to say you're happy? Oh, no, you're not happy. No." Montaviel shook his head. "That has nothing to do with you. Your emotion is satisfied, content with the face you want to place upon that. Are you happy? Nothing to do with you. No, you're not."

Alavan said, "We just have the same value for happiness as we do for crying. But we tend to put more value on one or the other. We tend to prefer happiness."

Montaviel continued, "They are identical. Limited control that we place on our own minds, not the expansiveness of what it's about. Always looking at the tiny picture, never the big one. The tiny one is easy. Our eyes don't have to go far." Alavan and Brent laughed. "The big one, whew, it's like too much. That's all the difference. But when you open your mind to let your higher consciousness let the spirit become the control of the universe, you don't have to do that anymore. You don't have to control anything."

Alavan said, "So, it's interesting that you can tell me that, and I can think that I know what you mean, but I don't."

Montaviel replied, "There's no way you can because you haven't reached that dimension to understand."

Alavan said, "And it's like, there's nothing I can do at this point that's going to change that. Whether I'm in the gutter or live in this house or with Somé, it doesn't matter."

Montaviel continued, "Talk about universal energies, universal thought. Save the forest, and we chop it down faster. Save the dolphins, and we kill them quickly. Save this, slaughter them." Montaviel shrugged. "Universal. Whether you slaughter them or you don't, you still have no control over whether they're here or not. You have no control. There wasn't one being on this planet when the dinosaurs were here. Uh oh, we had no control, and they're gone. What does that say about universal energy? Can't we look at just that one example and apply that to everything? Well, that's the way it was planned. That's how it was set up to be. Man, as who they are, has no control over anything, universally. Because they're all the same thing."

Alavan asked, "It's just the unveiling of our eyes to it?"

Montaviel replied, "Yeah, it's part of the dream."

Brent said, "Alavan? Knowing how strong you are..."

Alavan replied, "I don't know about that."

Brent continued, "I mean, just be honest with me. Be honest the best you can. If Somé were to leave, could you still be honestly happy?"

Alavan said, "I would be in grief for quite a while, without a doubt. And I wouldn't have the same levels of comfort or happiness that I have now but for quite a while. But, after all we've been through with you, with Spirit, everything I know, I just know that I would have to go on. There's no choice for me. I just know I would have to."

Brent replied, "You say you have no choice, yet..."

Alavan said, "That's the way I perceive it."

Brent continued, "That's the way you perceive it."

Alavan replied, "I mean, I could choose to be in misery about it, but I don't see that as something that... I mean, because he's going to die. I already know that."

Brent said, "I know, we're all going to die. I know, I know. I'm sorry. I can't. I can't make a choice right now."

Montaviel responded, "Way ahead of you. I'm not asking you to sit here and make a choice. I'm not asking you to do anything. That's not my job. I'm just stating facts."

A Higher Channel

Brent sighed, "I know."

Montaviel replied, "I'm just stating the realities of each choice. Every choice comes with a different reality. You can't hold the same reality for every choice. You just can't. With every movement your mind makes comes another choice and another reality. It happens so fast that you don't even see it happening. Yet you want to put so much emphasis on one tiny part. I understand that part of you, but I have to limit myself to such a tiny part of you to experience just that.

"And I have to block all the rest out. I can't see how you do that. I can see the possibilities from this reality, and a slightly bigger one, and even bigger. And the bigger the reality becomes, the more universal it becomes. You look back on your current reality, and you go, 'Oh my God, I had no idea that I could feel this way and see things this way. I thought this person held the key to my happiness.' You have that key, and you're the only one who has it. He doesn't have it. Somé doesn't have the key to your happiness." Montaviel pointed to Alavan. "He doesn't have it. I don't have it as part of you. I have no control over your happiness. It's right here." Montaviel pointed to his heart. "It belongs to you. It's only whether in your reality you want to experience it or not. That's a choice. That's all.

"Everything you'll ever be, you'll ever have, you'll ever know, is already embedded in your heart. And everything you feel, it's there. We just have to wash away all this stuff and get down to what we really feel inside. What do I want to be real in my life? What do I really see value in?

Do I see value in the essence of my soul and the emotion and richness of the experience I hold?

"Do I see value in that? Is there anything in that that holds the key to what may lie ahead? I would like to think, yes. I would really like to think yes. That holds a definite key because it's all in your heart. Never expect to find happiness in someone else." Montaviel shook his head. "It can't happen. It's an illusion. The illusion you paint in your mind for comfort, a false sense of security.

"It's not real. I can take you to people nearby right now, you know. Gladys and Bob in apartment 18, right next door. Gladys and Bob Richardson have been together for 27 years, right? 27 years. A long time. Is there a richness of experience? Neither one of them has experienced anything different except for three years out of 27. Three years is the only expansiveness of their relationship.

"But we look at them and go, 'Oh, isn't this sweet? Isn't this nice? Look at them. They've been together 27 years.' The guy's been dead for 24 years. He's a walking zombie."

Alavan asked, "Do you guys do anything with people like that? Tap on their head, or...?"

"40,000 times a day," Montaviel added with a chuckle. "And 40,000 times a day, another spirit comes around, putting disguises up, turning their heads. Oh, yeah. We never give up. It's our job." Alavan and Brent laughed.

Brent asked, "They've only experienced three years of the last 27 years?"

Montaviel replied, "The first three. The first three years of their companionship, if you want to call it that. Their togetherness. There was a richness of experience. It was impossible for them to experience any more past that time because of the limited reality they placed on themselves," Montaviel pointed to his head. "They're still living back in the sixties. They don't have any idea what's going on around them. But they are no more or no less than everybody else. But if you want to look at longevity, I can give you longevity as much as you want to see.

"But in almost every case of longevity, I will show you an empty heart. I will show you an empty soul. Why? Because we will not allow ourselves to expand our experience and our thoughts around that experience. I can also show you people who have been together over 50 years who in every one of those 50 years have grown and become separate within themselves, but together as one.

"And it's a beautiful thing to see. And I can show you more gay relationships than I can heterosexual ones that have more emotion, more feeling, and more experience than anywhere else on this planet. Anywhere else. Why? It's because the essence of togetherness is what makes it, and the limits of our own minds in a heterosexual relationship. There is an identity of being very separate from the beginning. You know, me Tarzan, you Jane."

Alavan said, "In straight relationships, There are more social stereotypes for them to follow, aren't there? There are more realities of other people that they can live by."

Montaviel replied, "The majority of heterosexual relationships, the learning experience of what they have, is completed in 72 hours."

Brent exclaimed, "No!??"

Montaviel nodded, "Completed. Now, if they're together one year, five years, 20 years, 50 years, the essence of the feeling within their heart is 72 hours. That's it."

"But does that diminish the whole thing? No, it just means that we have to wait a little more time before we can bring a different body into this existence, a different form so that their spirit can experience something a little different. And maybe it'll be 20, 30, 50, or 60 years in that existence, and maybe all they'll get is 72 hours.

"Maybe they'll get one week, maybe they'll get six years. Why do you think it takes so long to go through one experience, what we call one experience, the one experience of living in form? In a third-dimensional sense, we see millions of experiences. But in a fifth-dimensional sense, we're looking at one universal experience in this life form. Your spirit needs to gain this one experience. How long does it take for them to get this one? The average is 32,000 years."

Alavan asked, "And how many different incarnations?"

Montaviel replied, "Usually anywhere from two to as many as 2000."

Alavan said, "2,000 lives in form?"

Montaviel nodded and shrugged. "That doesn't mean anything."

Alavan laughed, "You've got nothing but time, huh?"

Montaviel said, "Exactly. But that really doesn't have any bearing on anything. I'm just saying that if we want to put a relative time frame in our limited way of thinking, there it is. But where are you in all of this? Well, you, the essence of you, your soul, is sitting back, waiting for the body to wake up so it can learn a little more. Let me learn a little more. Let me taste a new wine. You know, let's change from wine to champagne. What do you want to experience? Do you think your taste buds deserve more than you do? It's the way you treat yourself. You treat your forms in a third-dimensional sense as if the presence of God is in there. You should. But why can't the essence of your soul be treated like God? Why can't you treat it the same way that you treat your body? And that's really no different. It's still universal. It's still one thing. Yet, we treat ourselves to these things, but what is the soul doing? Sitting back in a Barcalounger or something?

"It's just waiting, waiting for the next moment the soul can grab and go, 'There's another learning experience I got. Hold on to that one.' Now we hold this one moment. Maybe in 20 years we'll get another one.'

And that's the way life is. Is there anything wrong with it? Nope. It's the way we're designed. So that's why I say the choices you make are the choices you make. It has nothing to do with anything. But we all want to put such vast importance on it."

Chapter 13: A Mother's Pride

Since we advertised in the local newspaper, we received many inquiries. One was from a realtor who said he had a house for sale that had been on the market for months. He said it should've sold immediately and was priced to sell. He wanted Somé to look at it. When asked for more information, he said that was all he had.

Somé felt that energy work would be needed, so he invited my brother to come along. Somé told us it was easier to move energy through a triangle of three people. Later, he would need no one else to help with the transfer.

When we pulled up in the driveway, we saw the house was white and surrounded by pine trees, which is common in the Monterey/Carmel area. It was a larger house by area standards. We met the realtor at the door. Somé stopped, closed his eyes, lowered his head, and then nodded as if to say his suspicions were correct. There were spirits in the house. He raised his hand with his eyes still closed and slowly opened and closed it as if feeling the energy from the door. He touched the door jamb, opened his eyes, nodded, and said, "Let's go in."

We entered the hallway, which included stairs to the second floor. Somé looked up the stairs and smiled, then his head snapped back to the hallway. He started walking down the hallway to the kitchen and, at each doorway, stopped and moved his head around with his eyes closed as if he were looking around. As we entered the first room, he looked toward a back corner and said, "There's one in here." As soon as the words left his mouth, he quickly turned his head to the right, where another doorway led to another room, and said, "He's fast." It seemed the spirit had zipped into the other room. Somé was mumbling something, but I couldn't make it out. He told me later he was talking to his higher spirit. He usually did this in another language from one of the stars from which his spirits are based. So, I could never make it out, but he asked them how to move these spirits to the fifth dimension as gracefully as possible. We stopped, and Somé had a little more conversation, positioned my brother and me in a small triangle, asked us to hold hands, and then said a few things I could not make out. I felt a rush of energy and then calm. Somé then said, "Let's go upstairs."

We walked up the stairs to the second floor, past a guest bathroom, and entered what looked to be the master bedroom. Somé's eyes were closed as he entered the bedroom. He stopped and smiled, his head bent down and tilted to the left. I could see his lips moving as if he was having a conversation, but I couldn't hear what was being said. He opened his eyes, smiled again, and said there was a woman there who had owned the house. She was waiting for her son to return. She asked if he would be returning soon. She also asked how her hair looked and if he would brush her hair. He also asked if there had been other people in this house, and she said there were, but that this was her house, and she was just waiting for her son to come back. Somé told her that her son was waiting for her, that he would take her to him, and that we would come back.

As we left the house and met up with the realtor, he said there was a fire some years ago and a woman had died in that very room. He said he hadn't mentioned it before because he wanted to see what Somé would come up with. After hearing that Somé recounted the exact events, the realtor asked if we could come back tomorrow, and we did. Alisal asked if more spirits might come by knowing that a portal would open. Somé answered, "Possibly."

We came back the next day and entered the lady's room. He talked to her a bit while we all stood together and held hands. Somé started the vortex of energy that she soon joined, reunited her with her son, and, according to Somé, two other spirits were transported as well. We heard later that the house sold very quickly after that.

There was another occasion when a woman called us to her house. She said that every time she walked into a particular room, she felt very cold and wondered if there was any energy causing this. The room was closed, and sheets covered much of the furniture. There were also many paintings on the wall and stacked on the floor. Somé closed his eyes and slowly turned his head as if scanning the room for abnormal energy. His head stopped, and he opened his eyes and slowly walked toward a stack of paintings on the floor leaning against the wall. He asked her what was in the stack. She said it was just some paintings. He asked if he could go through them. She said yes.

He quickly flipped through the pictures and then suddenly stopped at one. It looked like an oil portrait of a man likely painted in this century but not modern at all. Somé asked the woman, "Who is this?" She replied that it was the man who used to live here, and it was a self-portrait. Somé looked at it, closed his eyes, reopened them, and said, "He is in this painting."

Somé said a few words in a light tone with his eyes closed, smiled briefly, and then said, "It's done." He touched the doorway as we left and said, "Everything will be fine," smiled, and we walked away.

Back to the San Francisco session.

Alavan asked, "Same with the feelings?"

Montaviel replied, "Feelings are great to have. Very necessary to have."

Alavan said, "Just like when I'm having a good day and then, bam, something happens that tanks it."

Montaviel replied, "It's because it's part of the built-in mechanisms that tell you in your own mind that we have to feel bad part of the time. We can't feel good all the time. It's not real to be happy all the time."

Alavan said, "Well, isn't it also a part of life? Isn't it like you can't just cruise all day? But I think it's how you feel about how you feel or how you think about how you feel?"

Montaviel replied, "It's the reality base that you're working from that explains to you, that gives you a definition of what the feeling is. I can give you a thousand different realities with the same feeling, and you can think about the same feeling in a thousand different ways. That's not hard to do."

Alavan said, "You can feel bad and then feel bad about feeling bad. Or you can feel bad and say, 'Well, I feel bad right now.'"

Montaviel replied, "But most people are elated subconsciously about feeling bad." The group laughed. "Oh, this is the essence of their whole existence. This is the essence of their life, feeling bad." Brent laughed as if to acknowledge this was about him and motioned towards him.

Brent said, "Keep it coming, keep it coming."

Montaviel replied, "But you're no different than anybody else. Don't you think you're somebody special because you have the ability to do that. Oh, no. Everybody else has the same ability to do that."

Alavan said, "But most people would probably disagree if you told them that."

Montaviel replied, "Because their conscious mind tells them that they're not supposed to feel bad. See, this is the duality that you're always playing with, the duality in making your choice. If I do this, this will happen. If I do that, that will happen. Well, Jesus Christ!" Brent and Alavan laughed. "I wish you had the same determination in brushing your teeth in the morning as to what direction you should go. You know, if you dealt with that with the same determination and emotion, think of how your teeth would be. My God, we would have the healthiest teeth." Montaviel smiled.

Alavan said, "Actually, flossing is the key."

Brent agreed, "Yes."

Montaviel replied, "Well, whatever it is. You know, if you put everything that should be put in its proper order, everything would be dealt with identically. There's no difference. You can have a different feeling, you can have a different emotion, but it's dealt with exactly the same. It has to be. No different. And I know it's a reality that is very hard to comprehend, and it's a reality that is so foreign to most people that it's like, 'I don't understand what you're saying. I don't understand the feeling that I'm supposed to have.'

"Exactly true. We don't want you to have a feeling about that. We want you to be in the dark. Because being in the dark makes you search harder, go faster, and ask for clarification. And the minute things are clear, we push you into something else. That's what life is about."

Alavan asked, "So, would you say that path is about going where you usually don't go?"

Montaviel replied, "It's going where you've never gone."

Alavan continued, "That's what that path is about?"

Montaviel nodded. "That's what life is about."

A Higher Channel

Alavan said, "It's not about finding the safe spot or comfort zone. The happy place. It's about taking risks and going where you've never gone."

Montaviel replied, "Thinking about things you never thought of. A different reality base. And I cannot stress reality more than what I'm stressing here now. The ability to have anything you want in your life is just a flick of the finger away. But what reality base are you going to use with that? There is where your conflict," he pointed at Brent, "has always been and always will be. It will always be there."

"Why? It has to be. That's my job. It keeps you thinking; it keeps you moving forward. It keeps things fresh. You don't see it as fresh. I do. You don't."

Brent said, "Well, see, I don't see it as fresh because I don't see any happiness in life. In my mind, you know, if you're constantly..."

Montaviel interrupted, "You're turning it around. 'I don't see any happiness in life.' Well, what do happiness and life have to do with each other, to begin with? I said, in here," pointing to his heart, "if you have it in here, it's impossible, inconceivable, totally inconceivable, that when happiness is here," points at his heart again, "you can ever look out there and find anything more. It's not there. I have the love in here for myself. I have happiness here for myself. These things I have around me only add to my comfort in this closed environment that I'm in. They aren't the essence of my soul."

Alavan said, "And they don't necessarily make us eternally happy either." Montaviel shook his head. "Because once we acquire something like that, it shifts, and then we say, okay, we have this now, and now I want this, and I want that. I want something more."

Montaviel replied, "And your reality has to change constantly. It just doesn't work. It has to start right here, right inside of you. " He points to his torso. "It's there. Unlock it, let it out, and then it doesn't matter what goes on around you. It doesn't matter whose face is there because you've experienced that you hold the key to your own essence of your soul. You hold that key."

Alavan said, "You know what's funny? If you are truly searching for happiness, that's a logical step to take."

Montaviel replied, "Yourself."

Alavan asked, "Isn't it?"

Montaviel said, "Well, I would like to think so."

Alavan continued, "Because you can't lose it. You can lose a person, you know, you can lose a thing."

Montaviel replied, "You always, always will lose a person. You can't keep the person forever. You can keep the essence of your soul forever, up here." Montaviel pointed to his head. "The essence of your soul, the memory of what you hold in your soul and in your heart, remains with you for eternity. Can't get rid of that. You couldn't get rid of that if you tried. You can't. We're not made that way."

Alavan said, "You know, what's funny too is that it's actually the goal everybody has, even though they don't know it. Isn't that what you're doing here tonight? Kind of opening our eyes to that in a sense, saying, you know, this is actually what you're really looking for. It just looks like you're looking for it through this person or after this thing. But here's what you're really doing."

Montaviel replied, "What is the poor beggar in the street who has his little bottle of wine? That's his eternity of happiness. He's got that bottle of wine. You take that from him and he's more devastated than you are at this point. Because what will he do? He'll end his life. Why? Because you took his bottle of wine away. What does a bottle have to do with him? In the reality you work under, you would say, 'That's stupid.'

"It's inconceivable to think that the bottle of wine would be the controlling factor in his life. Oh, it's not inconceivable. And we support that just as much as we support you," to Brent, "or we support him," to Alavan. "We support every reality you have. And you keep us hopping. It's our job." Montaviel smiled.

"Don't be confused because there's no confusion. There is none. There really isn't. It's a very logical, understandable way for us to resolve everything. And the only thing I can say to you is that the choice is not yours and never has been yours. Yet we're letting you believe under your own guise of reality, your own illusion, that we're giving you this choice. The choice has already been predetermined as to what you're going to do. We already know what you're going to do."

Alavan said, "From now until eternity."

Montaviel nodded. "Yeah. Very few variations happen. Very few. In the way you think, there could be major differences. But no, they're just a little twist here and there to get everything back in order. It's not that big of a deal because we're working on universal energies and working on a whole universal energy. It's really easy to put, you know, 20 million people into one little group. And we can work on 20 million people in 3 seconds. It's not hard. Very easy. Because we're working with one energy, one thought distributed among 20 million, 50 million, or 1 billion. I don't care. One word is all it takes to trigger a response that we need to see in all these people".

"So, third dimensionally, the choice is yours. Fifth dimensionally, you have none. It's already done."

Brent said, "I feel bad or wrong."

Montaviel replied, "It's inconceivable. It's inconceivable to Spirit. It's inconceivable to the one that created us all. It's inconceivable to even think that anything's wrong. What's wrong? Nothing."

Alavan added, "And you shouldn't take anything that we say as thinking that you're wrong, because all we're doing is just saying, 'Oh, there's just a different way to look at it.' That's what he's doing. This is just another way to look at this."

Montaviel continued, "There are different ways of doing things. I can see within yourself, I can see probably about, let's say, 150, 150 different ways that you can take your life and the choices that you make, 150 different roads that you can travel. But guess what? All 150 roads go out." Montaviel spread his hands out. "And then they come right back to one. Someone else has 2000 roads, but they still come back to one."

Chapter 14: Disgruntled employee

We received a call from a local bar owner who wanted Somé to check out his bar because of some strange, unexplainable events. Things had disappeared, and weird noises were heard by cleaning crews and staff. We knew this bar well and had been there many times, as Monterey is a small town. It's the same bar where Somé learned about spirits, energy, and how people transfer them through projections.

Somé asked if we could come by during the day before the bar opened when it would be quiet with no music or disturbance. We scheduled an afternoon appointment for a couple of days later. He invited my brother to complete the triangle. We arrived in the middle of the day and approached the front door. Somé closed his eyes, touched the door entrance, opened his eyes, and we went in. It was dark in the main bar, even with the lights on. The bar was on the left with barstools and a large mirror behind it facing the floor. Tables were pushed to the side for cleaning, and the dance floor was straight ahead in the back. There was a door just past the dance floor that led to the back patio. It was very quiet inside as we were met by the owner and another worker.

The owner explained that there had been many odd disturbances, like loud noises, moving objects, and staff feeling uneasy for no good reason. He wondered if Somé could check if there was any energy behind it all.

A Higher Channel

Somé had already turned his head toward a corner of the room. When he asked what was there, the owner explained that it was a DJ booth behind the wall. Somé put his head down, slowly shook it from side to side, and mumbled a few words as if he were having a conversation. He began to nod his head in agreement with something. He said it was someone who used to work there and was upset about a few things.

The owner acknowledged that a former employee had passed away not too long ago and that the employee had worked there a long time. He did say things were a bit contentious toward the end. Somé recommended that we come back in a couple of days so he could do some prep work, and the owner agreed.

We came back a couple of days later. There were three of us, the owner and the current bar manager. Somé gave my brother and me explicit instructions to just focus on the energy movement and not react to anything we might see or hear. In fact, he said it was best to keep our eyes closed. He also brought some candles that we put in a large circle around us and lit them. Everyone was given the same instructions, but the bar manager struggled to follow them.

We were all seated on the dance floor, and Somé indicated that he was beginning and asked us to close our eyes and focus on loving energy. He would do the rest. Just a few seconds later, the bar manager started yelling out loud, "You son of a bitch! You have no right to do this!" and other complaints. He was yelling at the spirit of the person who had passed away and continued to haunt them. He continued until Somé exclaimed, "Stop!" The owner also asked the manager to be quiet. We sat for a few more seconds, and I felt a wind blow across my face; then, we heard a rumbling sound that clanged some glasses and bottles together. This was strange as there were no doors or windows open to the outside. As the breeze passed, I heard Somé take a couple of deep breaths and then say, "It is done. He won't be bothering anyone anymore, but he did ask that I share something with the owner that only the owner can hear." With that, Somé and the owner walked outside into the back part of the bar to discuss what was said. He never shared with me what was said as it was private and between those two. We heard from the owner later that everything was back to normal, and the incidents had ceased.

Back to the San Francisco session.

Montaviel said, "I don't care what you do with your life. I don't care. It has no effect on anything. You've already gone down 150 roads. Why aren't you thinking about those 150 roads as much as you're thinking about this one that has just passed? You've taken a detour. What's wrong with the other 150? What is wrong with the, you know, 3000 people that you had a direct effect on in another country?

"Why isn't there any thought placed on that? Because you've moved on, which you should have. You are a different person today than you were then. We are working under a different reality. So, you can look back at that and have the memory of certain things. But to know that 3000 people were directly affected by your presence there, and you thought you lost. You thought it was a useless part of what you did. Nothing of what you do is useless. Nothing. Nothing.

"In one lifetime, the average person affects 17 million people. How? You think, how?" Montaviel grabbed his head to mimic confusion. "How can I affect 17 million people in my lifetime? That's just the average. Somé has already affected 350 million people. 350 million people. You think, 'No, that's impossible.' It's only impossible because you're limited in how you think. No, it's not impossible. And he doesn't do anything compared to a lot of other people. Nothing. But the effect of what he does ripples.

"One thought ripples into a tidal wave on the other side of the universe. It gets bigger, bigger, bigger. That's what thought does. That's what the essence of who you are in this life form today does. It's a rippling effect of experiences, and the richness of each experience you have sends a tidal wave at the end of your life existence. It's a tidal wave. It's a tidal wave into spirit from the rippling effect of everything you've gone through.

"But we keep ourselves enclosed in one little experience only. We take so long to get that ripple into a wave and that wave into the explosion at the end."

Brent said, "I know you know this already, but it's like, I find it so upsetting that the one time in my life that I'm able to finally feel this, after all these experiences I've had and everything, I just want to know..."

Montaviel replied, "You want to know why? You want to know why you feel stronger about this one than anything else you've had?"

Brent said, "Well, it's just, yeah, I want to know why, but I want to know why I have to give it up so that it's just another experience and move on to another one and another one. I'm tired of that."

Montaviel said quietly, "Who said that you have to do that? No one is saying that you have to do that."

Brent replied, "I know, but I know I have this choice set before me. It's right there. But by making this choice, I have to also accept the fact that he's going to get up and leave again."

Montaviel said, "It's possible. The possibility is there. Sure. And the possibility for it not to be there is also there. But how else can you gauge your choice? How can you gauge your choice by painting an illusion of fantasy that's not there yet or by looking at what you know positively to be true?

"Now, what reality do you want to go on when you're choosing this one entity to be part of your life? When you choose one thing, do we look at what might happen? Everyone else does. They look at, well, yeah, I'm going to give this another try because it's going to be different. Well, can it be? Oh, sure. But it can only be different if you're different." Montaviel gestured toward Brent.

"It can only be different if he's different. That's the only difference. We can't work under the same reality. It has to be different realities. We have no control over that. You do. At least we give you the illusion that you do." Montaviel looked at Alavan. "It's kind of an endless battle. It really is." Brent shrugged in frustration. "And I understand why it is. And I'm not trying to diminish how you feel. I'm not trying to belittle you in any way whatsoever. I'm just trying to let you, for a small moment, understand that the importance you place on everything is real only by one reality standpoint, by one."

Brent said, "I'm thankful for the experience I had with Michael, right? It was beautiful. It was a wonderful experience. But I don't, I don't want to have to do that. You know, I..."

Montaviel replied, "So far, that's good..."

Brent continued, "I want to be comfortable; you know that. You know, the intimacy is a big part for me."

Montaviel said, "Yes, it should be."

Brent said, "I can't. I can't do that. I can't be intimate with all these different people."

Montaviel replied, "True."

Brent continued, "Especially in the world now, you know? And so that's another big reason why, you know, I want to be with one person. I know that with that one person, we could be together without having to worry about that. You know, I can't. I don't like this whole idea of going out and sure, you feel good about somebody and then going home, but you can't do anything."

Montaviel asked, "So, what do you want to do about that?"

Brent replied, "I'm just saying this is another reason I want Alisal back. Because that's another comfort."

Montaviel said, "Okay."

Brent continued, "That's another aspect of having a long-standing relationship with one person. You can't jump around."

Montaviel replied, "Okay."

Brent said and fidgeted in his chair, "You know..."

Montaviel said, "Number one, nobody's asking you to jump around. It was never talked about jumping around. I'm just saying the vastness of the experience is there, whether it's with one person or 100,000."

Brent sighed and replied, "I know."

Montaviel continued, "Which you would never be able to experience because there isn't that much time left in your life to experience 100,000."

Brent said, "I know that, but..."

Montaviel said, "But what I'm saying is that the emphasis you're putting on one thing is not the controlling factor of who you are.

"And as long as you understand that, then choices are very easy to make. Very easy to make. They're not hard to make. But don't expect to have a different reality, a different conscious working reality on the same experience. I don't know where I'd find it. I can't create that; you can't create that."

Brent asked, "Can I go… Can I make the decision to have Alisal back in my life, but go in with the things that I have learned? Or am I just going to fall back?"

Montaviel replied, "What do you think you're going to do? You already know, you already know what you're going to do."

Brent said, "I would like to go in with what I've learned, right?"

Montaviel replied, "You would do that. You would most definitely do that. But what would happen?"

Brent said, "I don't know. I don't know."

Montaviel asked, "So, what's the problem with the decision, then? You have just as much not knowing within your mind right now in that relationship as you do in not having the relationship. And in going into a different reality of the expansion of yourself, there's just as much fear and unknowing as there is in something that you claim not to know. The illusion has already been painted in front of your face in this relationship. So, it's like, 'I want to go in with a new experience that I have.' Beautiful. Wonderful. I mean, very realistic in how your reality is painting the picture. Very realistic. I'm not trying to diminish that. But once another element is brought into it, new realities are brought into it.

"And what do new realities do to you? They wash away every beautiful and perfect intent you have. They wash them away.

"Why? Because you don't have it here to begin with." Montaviel pointed to his own heart. "If you have it here, to begin with, no one in the universe can wash anything away. If I had that within you right now, I would have no problem seeing anything. I still don't have a problem. But in your sense, having a problem, you can clearly see what you have.

"You can clearly see what the other person will offer in your life. You can see things as clear as day, things that are meant to be seen. So, I'm saying, have all the hope in the world. Life is based on it. That's who we are. You can never be without hope. Hope is a wonderful thing. But as your reality about yourself changes, as your ideas about yourself change, and as the wholeness starts to appear and the comfort of loving yourself is there, choices have to change, and they will change.

"But it could still be the same person. It could still be the same person. So, the hope and everything you want to do is there. I'm just saying, look at the whole picture at once. Don't take little parts that you want to look at.

Don't exclude the essence of the whole energy by only focusing on the little things.

"Look at the whole picture. Look at yourself. Am I emotionally secure in who I am and how I feel to be able to go through and do whatever it takes to bring this person back into my life? Until that answer becomes a reality to you, I wouldn't place anybody in my life. Nobody.

Brent said, "Okay."

Montaviel replied, "And that's as clear as it's going to get."

Brent said, "That's the clearest answer that I have got. It seems like, not that you haven't tried, but that right there just said more for me."

Montaviel responded, "My job is to not make things really hard." Brent laughed. "You can thank Somé for that last part. Because the last part is more of what he would say than what I would say, but the essence of it is the same."

Brent said, "I like that better."

Montaviel replied, "He knew you would. It has, um, what he says, 'feeling'. It has meaning."

Brent said, "Well, it just gives me a little more sense of hope."

Montaviel said, "And that's not wrong to have."

Brent replied, "I'm just saying that, yeah."

Montaviel said, "I just don't want you to..."

Brent interrupted, "Don't put somebody else there until I'm ready."

Montaviel said, "Exactly. And we wouldn't."

Brent continued, "I don't know. That just rang clearer than anything. And I don't mean to diminish you at all."

Montaviel replied, "You can't. Inconceivable." Alavan and Brent laughed. "You have to understand that once you reach a point within yourself, this is the beauty of yourself, the beauty of everybody. To be in a life form, like you are now, and with an expansive reality to work from, and to know that you are the essence of the universe. You are everything. You are every thought, every breath of air, every touch, every smell. Everything is a part of you in that expansiveness. There is just so much. Don't limit yourself. Don't do that. Don't limit yourself to being happy with one part of yourself. Be fierce. Be demanding. Be demanding as hell. You deserve it all. And we won't stop until you get it all. We can't. It's our job.

"You'll get it. I know you will. You can't not. But easy? No." Montaviel shook his head. "And you are so much already on that path. So much, so much more than you let yourself believe."

Brent said, "I'm the type that just doesn't give credit to myself for much of anything."

Montaviel replied, "I know. But you're there. Just stop, stop the war within yourself. It's not necessary. It's not going to change anything. It just slows your thinking process and keeps you in your little confined environment, the way you think.

"We're not saying that that's wrong. I'm just saying that there is something else out there. A lot of something else. And you can experience so much of it being in a life form. My God, you can experience so much more than what you experience now. And fear doesn't have to be a part of it. Worry doesn't have to be a part of it. It doesn't have to be a part of it.

"If you choose to, sure, it can be a part of it. And even when I think of all the people that you would consider being on this higher dimensional plane of thinking from their higher consciousness, from all of us up here, even those people, you don't understand what they go through in their minds and even in their clarity of how they describe things. They still create little obstacles, little things. They create little things to worry about. But instead of having them as what you would consider big significant worry events, they're tiny little things, insignificant things, but they keep it in perspective. However, they still have the built-in mechanisms of being limited.

"See, just because you're limited here in what you can physically do does not limit this." Montaviel pointed to his head. "Unlimited, it goes on. It goes on forever. Once the creation of your soul and your spirit was created, there's no taking that back. Done. Now, it's just gaining experience. And how you want to gain experience is fine. Right now, we have people that come into these life forms like this to where we can explain different ways of collecting experience. That's all it is about."

Montaviel continued, "I don't see a lot of emotion in that. I see a lot of beauty in that, but I sure don't see any emotion. I don't see a problem. But you can create a problem, and you can create a problem faster than what I can see is not there. It's just instantaneous within your mind. The problem is there. Why? It's part of that mechanism. But we let that mechanism work repeatedly to keep us confined to small places in small boxes.

"We keep ourselves from even exploring the possibility of doing something different. It's not necessary. It serves no purpose in your experience. Serves no purpose. And why? Lesson number 2, four hours ago: The experience has nothing to do with me. The experience is separate from me."

Alavan asked, "What do we take from the experience that makes the difference?"

Montaviel replied thoughtfully, "When you take from the experience, you take the essence of going through it, the experience itself."

Alavan considered this and asked, "And the way that your moods and feelings changed and how you related to it?"

Montaviel shook his head slightly. "Not so much your feeling. The experience. The act of the experience, not the emotion we had for it. The physical act of going through an experience is the physical act of going through the experience in form. That's why spirit is placed into form. The physical experience gives your spirit the knowledge," he said, pointing to his head. "The understanding."

Alavan still seemed curious. "I'm just wondering, what about the experience takes hold? Is it the visual part? Is it an energy exchange that's different? Is it different than how you would have felt had you not had the experience?"

Montaviel explained, "Most experiences that people have are more in thought than anything else. You can experience more things per day in thought than you can ever experience in physical form."

Alavan nodded slowly. "It's like we think of doing something and then stop and say, 'No, I just don't want to do that.'"

Montaviel explained, "It's about the experience. You combine the physical part—the sight, the smell. The essence of the experience is what gets passed on to your soul, your spirit."

He continued, "You can't understand the essence of anything until you look inside yourself. You have to go deep inside. It's not about the superficial things we see. We think picking up gadgets and doing tasks are part of the experience, but they're not. The real experience of life is different from all these things," he said, gesturing to various objects around them. "But we try to make these things part of our experience, and that's where the confusion comes in. We think, 'I need to have this.' But why did people go through life 16,000 years ago without this stuff? Why could they do it back then?"

Chapter 15: Aloha

The years following the early 90s took us in many directions. I remember attending a psychic fair in Monterey. A woman there was doing readings, and she seemed pleasant, so Somé sat down. She took his hand, stared at his palm, closed her eyes, and opened them. She said, "It feels like our roles should be reversed, and you should be doing this for me." We all chuckled. She continued, saying she sensed a lot of spiritual support for Somé and that he connected to multiple sources.

There was also an aura detector machine at the fair that I wanted to try. I sat in a chair, placed my hand on a receptacle, and a few seconds later, an image of me with a surrounding aura was printed. Somé wanted to try it, too and said he would send energy through the receptacle to see how it would show up in his aura. Well, the machine stopped working. They didn't know how or why, but they couldn't print an image for Somé.

Another odd experience in Monterey happened at the aquarium. When we walked by the dolphin exhibit, two gray dolphins were swimming by. They suddenly stopped, turned vertically, and floated underwater while staring at us. I asked Somé what they were doing, and he said, "They sense your energy." It was as if they recognized something familiar and wondered what it could be on the other side of the transparent wall.

We moved north of San Francisco from Monterey to Monte Rio, a small town on the Russian River. We rented one of eight casitas owned by

Bob and Israel, who had a house overlooking the river. There were nine casitas, with six facing each other and a rock pathway and beautiful garden between them. I found temporary work in Santa Rosa, the largest nearby city, about a 30-minute drive away. My brother Alisal, who worked in a San Francisco hotel, rented one of the other casitas even though it was a 90-minute commute to that city.

We spent only a few months in Monte Rio, but I remember some of Somé's nephews visiting. One of them, Tom, was a paranoid schizophrenic. Even though he had medication to help him, voices in his head were constantly telling him what to do. Tom was over for dinner one night, and we were chatting about random spiritual stuff when Tom clearly became agitated. Somé and I both wondered if he was hearing chatter. Tom kind of chuckled. Somé then said, "It isn't true. What they're telling you isn't true."

Tom asked, "You can hear them?"

Somé replied, "Yes – they said that we were liars, out to get you and should be killed."

"Holy shit – you're right! How do you know that?" Tom replied.

"It's just a little gift that I've been given," Somé said.

I asked, "That's a pretty intense conversation. Are they always like this?" Tom said that they were but that the medication kept them at bay. He said he just ignores them normally, but they make him laugh. It was late, and Tom left. We never saw him again, but we heard he was doing well.

After a few months in Monte Rio, my brother Somé and I moved to Hawaii. Why not? We had no jobs, less than $2,000 after selling everything in a two-day garage sale, and eight pieces of luggage. So, off we went for a one-week stay at a hotel in Waikiki Beach. After that, we just winged it. Alisal got a job bussing tables in a restaurant, bringing home cash each night. I got a teller job at a Savings and Loan in downtown Honolulu, and Somé got a job taking tickets at a parking garage and doing security detail at night.

We bounced around short-term rentals in Waikiki until we finally found a home in Manoa, where we rented the bottom half of an old two-story house. Manoa, just outside Honolulu, was beautiful and seemed to rain a lot. The weather patterns varied widely on such a small island due to the topography and mountain ranges. We loved getting to know the locals, their customs, their big hearts, and their willingness to bring you into their family. You are instantly an "auntie" or "uncle" to their kids, and potlucks are all the rage. In our short 2.5 years there, we learned how to slow down and appreciate the small things in life.

Somé and I attended a "walk-in" event on Maui in 1994. Even though the female person was different now and the male hosted an entirely new walk-in, much of the messaging was similar to their books, tapes, and past events. It felt almost like a reunion and a communion of kindred spirits.

Somé continued to set up energy portals in all the places we visited in Hawaii, but he mentioned that the activity in these portals was much less than on the mainland. He also discovered that the Polynesian and Asian people who lived there had reincarnated over a more extended period, from 50,000 up to 200,000 years. The average on the mainland was about 40,000 years.

I remember we had a roommate in Manoa named Adrian, who was a hairstylist at the Ala Moana mall. One night at the dinner table, as we got to know each other, Somé started talking about Adrian's past and connections. He said Adrian was mainly connected to his mom and Somé could help him by clearing some of the old energy that had been with him for a while. It was routine for Somé now, who would say a few things in his head to get things going, and most spirits would go quietly. However, this time, the last spirit did not want to go and had very choice words for Somé. This spirit used every cuss word in the book, yelling and being very foul-mouthed, according to Somé. Undeterred, Somé continued the process, and the final spirit was escorted out. Adrian felt a little dizzy, but it soon cleared up. He said he had a clarity he hadn't had for a long time. This usually lasts a couple of days, but it doesn't take long for the old realities to need support again. However, the overall intensity was less this time, and Adrian found that taking the next steps was a little easier each time.

A Higher Channel

We left Hawaii and returned to the mainland, staying with friends in San Francisco. Alisal followed, and we eventually met Brent there as well. We moved into the Castro district in San Francisco, probably the liveliest gay area in the city at the time. Somé continued to set up portals in some of the most energetically active bars. We enjoyed our time there, especially playing pool and pinball while downing beers at the Moby Dick, one of the oldest gay bars in the area.

Back to the San Francisco session.

Alavan pondered, "But we do things to take us out of our pain and feelings, don't we?"

Montaviel shook his head. "No, you do more to create pain because pain is pleasure. Pain and sorrow are pleasures. That's how our mechanism works."

Brent laughed, "Maybe Joseph, your colleague, is on the right track with that S&M reference—pain is pleasure."

Montaviel smiled. "Sounds self-inflicted and personal, not quite the same."

Alavan asked, "What's your take on that? I don't understand it because it's not part of my experience."

Montaviel replied, "Well, it was. Just because it isn't right now doesn't mean it wasn't part of your experience."

Alavan conceded, "At some point, yeah, I suppose."

Montaviel challenged him, "Are you so much better than what the whole universe holds?"

Alavan conceded, "No, you already know that. No, no."

Montaviel continued, "Everything you see, hear, and have done or not done is still part of your experience. Just because you don't participate now doesn't mean that experience isn't yours. It belongs to you as much as it does to those doing it. Your reality base is just different from theirs. But is what they're doing any better or worse than your thoughts about it? No. Experience is experience. But how much emotion do we want to throw into it? We can add fear and confusion and say, 'I can't think. I can't operate because I'm thinking about these people hurting themselves.'"

He nodded. "You can do it. You can do anything in thought that you want. Create any feeling you want. It's your choice."

Alavan asked, "Why don't people want to be alone?"

Montaviel shook his head. "It's a built-in mechanism."

Alavan agreed, "Yeah. Like, if I'm feeling lonely, I jump on the computer or watch TV. We do everything to avoid it."

Montaviel explained, "Even people who claim to be reclusive have a greater need for being around others than those who are always around people."

Alavan wondered, "What are they doing when they're by themselves?"

Montaviel said, "They read, they watch TV. They do different things."

"Are they miserable?" Alavan asked.

"No, no," Montaviel assured. "They have more people around them than you do when you're out with people."

"Really? In their mind?" Alavan asked.

"They can watch a show and see 300 people. That's part of their experience. That's part of their life. They don't need to meet others to gain experience. They can see it through this," he pointed at the TV. "Your reality says they're not gaining experience, but they definitely are, just as much if not more than you."

Alavan nodded, "We've talked about that how TV and movies can give you an experience just by watching."

Montaviel agreed, "Yes because they place themselves in a protective reality shield. They don't take in outside energy from people. They gain experience and feel safe in their own minds. They control their environment this way. They experience different people but lack the essence of the experience itself. They gain a lot of information but not the essence unless it's done with another person."

Brent asked, "What about people without TV or phones, like those off in the mountains? Are they getting it through nature?"

Montaviel nodded, "Yes, that's the essence of who they are."

Brent added, "It's everything that surrounds them, away from it all."

"They're not alone," Montaviel agreed.

Brent echoed, "They're not alone."

Montaviel concluded, "Alone is a funny concept. In my reality, alone has no meaning. When you say alone in a fifth-dimensional sense, I can't see where that possibility exists. So, in your reality, words like alone bring back a memory."

Alavan asked, "So, you can relate?"

Montaviel said, "I can relate to being alone, but I don't value it."

Brent added, "Yeah, well, John Bradshaw, the author, said that the only people who feel loneliness are those who love. If someone isolates themselves in nature, away from other humans, they won't feel lonely because everything they love is right there and can't be taken away."

Montaviel nodded. "These people have true love in their hearts. Sharing that love with nature, flowers, grass, or animals is just as fulfilling as sharing it with another person. In fact, it might be even more gratifying because they already have that love inside them." He pointed to his heart.

"But we tend to see things from our own perspective and expect everyone else to fit into our little box."

Alavan agreed, "We've talked about that before—misery loves company. If you're feeling down, you want to bring someone down with you."

Montaviel nodded. "You make sure someone goes along with you."

Alavan continued, "And if you're mad at someone, you want them to feel bad too. You take your revenge, and then you feel better."

Montaviel explained, "Energetically, you've just passed it on to someone else, as long as they're willing to take it. And most people are willing to take anything you dish out."

Alavan nodded. "Typically, you know what pushes their buttons."

Montaviel said, "This is what I mean by manipulation. It's your way of manipulating."

"Yeah," Alavan agreed.

Montaviel smiled. "Manipulation is the essence of being in human form," Brent and Alavan laughed. "But many people don't want to think they're manipulating."

Alavan added, "Or destroying. They don't want to be seen as destroyers."

"Destroyer is an easy term. I'd rather use something like murderer," Montaviel said with a laugh. "That's the essence of what you're doing."

"Taking life?" Alavan asked.

"Killing, murder—energetically, it's the same. You manipulate, you murder, you deceive, and these are the essences of life," Montaviel explained.

Alavan asked, "What about lying? We lie."

Montaviel shook his head. "That's a very third-dimensional perception. There are no lies. It's impossible to lie. There's no essence for lying. It's just a concept you place on something that doesn't fit your reality. It doesn't fit your picture or how you think; it's a lie."

Alavan pondered this. "What about when we tell Spirit that we want to be with someone who can be honest, who doesn't lie? What do we do with that?"

Montaviel replied, "All I hear when you ask that is 'honest' and 'me.' I don't need to hear anything else. So, I bring honesty out within you because I can't bring it out in someone else. When you ask for someone honest, it means you need to feel honesty here first," he said, pointing to his heart, "before you can attract it from someone else."

He continued, "Why do certain people come into your life? Because that's the essence of who you are. This is the energy you're working with.

You can't expect anything more. When someone doesn't fit your new picture, it's because you changed the picture. So, we take that person out and search for someone who fits your new picture. We didn't change the picture—you did. Now you're kicking yourself for it. But that's what life is about. Life is about trying everything."

Montaviel looked down at the ashtray, holding what was left of his cigarette. "And it's going to hit, believe me, it's going to hit with a bang. There's no way it can't."

Montaviel changed subjects to the cigarette debacle in his hand. "I didn't know what Some needed, but I was setting things on fire, " he said, which made everyone laugh.

"It doesn't matter. It's in the ashtray," Alavan said, chuckling.

Montaviel added, "He told me I was sloppy anyway, whatever that means."

"Tell him I didn't know he could smell out of form," Alavan joked.

In a quieter tone, Montaviel said, "It's very difficult to embed a reality that everyone else sees, but you don't. If it's not difficult, don't accept it. Don't accept a reality that comes easy. You've already done it if you understand it and it comes easy. It doesn't matter what form it takes or how familiar it seems. If it comes easy, it's not real. It's an illusion you paint for yourself. We're good at seeing what we want to see. You have to see it before you look for it. Instead, look for it in your soul, mind, and dreams.

It becomes so real that it's embedded right here," he pointed to his torso. "Then you give up control. Energy pulls like a magnet right to you. If another person is going through the same process, there can be an even stronger magnetic pull between the two of you. But don't let your old reality and emotions determine what's best for you. You have to know in your heart, your soul, and your mind. You have to know. You have to feel the essence of your love, of everything you are. You have to feel that, know that it's there so that when things happen in your life, you can't be so readily affected emotionally, psychologically, and mentally. The effect isn't there because you can't take this away," he patted his heart. "It's right here. It's all I need to have."

Montaviel then turned his head to talk to Somé and said something indistinguishable.

"What did he say?" Alavan asked.

"It's time to stop," Montaviel replied.

"Okay," Alavan agreed.

Montaviel continued, "I know I gave you more than you can think about right now, and the confusion is still there, maybe even more so. But I want the confusion to be there. I would pray to keep the confusion there. I don't want you to see clearly. Not now. The confusion is your mechanism for yourself."

Alavan reflected, "That's where that quote came in. Someone once said, 'You're at your best when things are the worst.'"

"It's true," Montaviel confirmed.

Brent added, "Well, it is during those times that I feel the strongest. During those times, I come to Somé and ask him to tell me, you know."

"You can't change that part of you," Montaviel stated.

"When Alisal was in Tulsa, I needed that, you know," Brent said.

"And times like that will happen over and over again. Embrace the confusion and uncomfortability because it's the essence of your soul. That's what we're dealing with. We're not dealing with another person; we're dealing with the essence of your soul. You." He furrowed and then relaxed his brow. "And me." Everyone laughed.

Brent quoted, "You just spoke the words in that song from Ace of Base, 'I will not say sorry for the essence of my soul.'"

"How can you?" Montaviel smiled. "You didn't create it; it was given to you. That's the gift. It's a wonderful gift. No, you don't make excuses for the essence of who you are."

"Thank you," Brent said.

"Yeah, thank you for coming. It was really nice having you," Alavan added.

"It's been quite an experience," Montaviel nodded. "More than you realize right now. Quite a life-changing experience for you and your reality. Thank you."

"Thank you again," Alavan and Brent echoed.

Montaviel bowed his head and took deep breaths. His brow furrowed, and his abdomen contracted and expanded. His face grimaced as emotion spread through his body, and he inhaled sharply as if crying. He gasped, covered his face, and sobbed. Both hands covered his face as Somé returned to his own body. He wiped his eyes, and Brent rubbed his back to make sure he was okay. Somé finished wiping his eyes as they continued to tear up.

"Oh, I need a cup of coffee. Real bad," Somé said, making everyone laugh.

"Hey, babe. Be careful when you stand up. You've been sitting there a while," Alavan stated.

"I need to wipe down this table. I kept asking him to," Somé said.

"I could tell he was listening to you, but getting him to do something was another matter," Alavan replied as Somé cleared his throat and coughed a few times.

"Oh, I'm glad you got that last part of Somé coming back in on the video," Alavan said as Brent brought Somé coffee.

"Oh yeah," Brent agreed.

"Does it seem long to you when you're out?" Alavan asked Somé.

"No," Somé replied.

"How long did it seem?" Alavan asked.

"Ten minutes," Somé said.

"Really?" Alavan asked in surprise.

"Yeah," Somé confirmed.

"Well, we filled three 2-hour tapes," Brent noted.

"What time is it?" Somé looked at the clock. "Sheesh, it's one o'clock in the morning. One o'clock???"

"Yeah, can you believe it?" Brent asked.

"What time did we start?" Somé inquired.

"Seven," Brent replied.

Somé coughed, saying, "I told him to cough, and he wouldn't."

Alavan replied, "He did a couple of times. He coughed up phlegm." As Somé stood up slowly and straightened his back, Alavan asked, "What's the emotion you go through when you come back in? Is it just the way it happens to your body?"

Brent interrupted, "Oh, I see something."

"What?" Somé asked.

Brent leaned in. "I just want to look at your eyes."

"Why?" Somé questioned.

Alavan chimed in, "Is it different?"

Brent observed, "Yeah, the difference is your eyes are really dilated. I just want to see what happens when; you know..."

Alavan added, "Oh. He had a whole different look. I mean, your face is different. Everything's different. Not totally, but your expressions are different."

Somé explained, "Well, you have to remember that body parts are universal. So, when someone else, as he put it, the essence of the energy of someone else, is there and they're used to doing things automatically differently than what you do."

Alavan laughed, "He really didn't know how to smoke a cigarette."

Somé continued, "When you talk about someone else being there, I don't look at myself in the face. I listen more to what's being said. So, I don't see what you see. I don't even see that as myself because I am myself. Even though the look is there, I don't look at the look. I listen to the voice more than anything else. The look has no relevance because I'm me. I just don't happen to be in that body that you think is me. It's so hard to describe."

He paused and then said, "So, when you say my eyes look different, or I have a different expression, or maybe the way I say something is different, it's different because even though I'm using the same things that I have, a lot of it is going to be the same because this is me. They're using me, but many little things should be different because it's different, you know?"

Brent added, "One thing I noticed is that during that whole time, you know how you stutter a little bit."

Somé agreed, "Oh, yeah, quite a bit."

Alavan interjected, "He did it once, towards the beginning. I made a note to myself that stuttering is part of his form. He didn't do it as much as Somé did, but he did it once. It's a form thing."

Brent nodded, "It's something that's in his spirit. It was right at the very start. Well, Spirit was uncomfortable, just coming into the form."

Alavan continued, "Yeah. Well, there were a lot of things that were different. See how he started to relax after a while?"

"Oh, yeah," Brent agreed.

Chapter 16: The Final Journey

We lived in San Francisco for a couple more years. In 1996, the San Francisco Board of Supervisors passed an ordinance allowing public officials to perform domestic partnership rites for any two people who register with the city. In March, we were one of 165 gay and lesbian couples recognized in a public ceremony as domestic partners. It was a historic day.

I worked for a body piercing company in the city and later got an accounting job for a real estate development company in the Embarcadero. Somé, who was 25 years older than me, quit working while we were in Hawaii.

In the late '90s, the real estate developer I worked for started building apartment complexes in Phoenix, Arizona, and offered me a chance to move there to support the projects. We bought a house in an old historic district, joined bowling and dart leagues, made many friends, and enjoyed life in Phoenix. Somé developed COPD after a lifetime of smoking and was advised to move to an area with cleaner air.

In 2004, we moved to San Diego, where I got a job with a communications provider. Somé and I were married on June 18, 2008, just two days after same-sex marriage licenses were made available in San Diego. Proposition 8 would ban same-sex marriages again in November 2008, although our marriage license would continue to be valid. It would be another 5 years before gay marriage was legal again in California. We lived there until I received a promotion and transferred to Georgia in 2018.

Somé continued to set up energy portals everywhere we went. We often talked about Spirit. He would channel occasionally for close friends or provide guidance. We spent time with his kids and grandchildren almost every year. He reconnected with his brother and sisters and was grateful for the connections and time spent with his family.

In mid-December of 2022, Somé was experiencing pain in his chest, so I took him to the Emergency Room. They tested him for a heart attack, which came back negative, and they admitted him. He had a lot of fluid that had built up around his left lung, which they eventually extracted. All the other tests came back negative, but he still experienced a high level of pain in his chest area. He was discharged, and I brought him home after picking up a prescription for morphine, as traditional painkillers did not help.

Over the next few days, he slept a lot, often waking for food and drink or to play his computer games for a few minutes before falling asleep again. I brought him out one morning to his favorite reclining chair to watch TV and I found it odd that he wasn't asking for any pain medications, but I just figured that the morphine was doing its job better than the prior medications had done. At one point, he woke up from a nap and said that he had to pee. I asked if he could get up so that I could help him into his electric scooter to go to the bathroom. He replied that he was unable to do so. I asked him if he could stand up. He said, 'No'. Unsure if he was extra tired or needed some more rest, I just let him be, covered up with his favorite blanket. Several hours passed, and he woke up exclaiming, 'There's no air! We need more air!'. I checked the oxygen machine and the air output, and everything worked fine. This exclamation didn't seem like him, but I told him everything checked out, and he fell asleep.

I woke him up after another couple of hours and asked him, "Can you get up yet?" He shook his head no. I replied, "Babe, it seems your body is being prepared for the transition." I asked him as my voice started to quiver.

"It has already begun," he replied softly.

I began sobbing. I knew what this meant and had prepared myself for years for this moment, but nothing really can prepare you for the realization that someone is in the process of dying right in front of you.

Over the next several hours, I watched him from my chair, wondering what to do. I noticed he began to smile as if he was dreaming of something wonderful, but I'd never seen him smile in his sleep before. I cried, happy for him but sad that this was finally the end of our life together.

I called an ambulance the next morning to take him to the hospital, as I wanted him to be as comfortable as possible. He woke up when they got there, and they lifted him and wheeled him out of the house.

A Higher Channel

They took him to the ER and got him to bed. He was fairly lucid when they asked for his name and date of birth and asked him if he had any pain. He said that he did not. After the doctor faced away and typed on a keyboard, Somé looked at me, waved goodbye, and said, "I love you."

"I love you, too," I replied with tears and ran over and hugged him.

As they wheeled him upstairs to a hospital bed, I could tell that Somé was gone, but another spirit was in his place for the final transition. He had a very different personality but could answer all the same questions when asked by the nurses. He was pretty cantankerous and distrustful of me and the nursing staff. Anytime we tried to offer something to him, he would scowl and say, "I know what you're trying to do." It was bizarre, but I had to roll with the process.

After the nurses left and I sat down in the chair beside him, several hours passed before Somé took his last breath on December 25, 2022, at 80 years old. We had an amazing journey, and I cherish every moment. I will never forget him, what Spirit gave us, and our experiences together. His impact will be felt for millennia, as all of our impacts will be felt. I am forever grateful.

A Higher Channel

Alavan (left) and Somé (right) in Amalfi, Italy 2015

Bibliography

Millman, Dan. *Way of the Peaceful Warrior: A Book That Changes Lives*. J.P. Tarcher, 1980.

Dyer, Dr. Wayne W. *How To Be A No-Limit Person*. Simon & Schuster. 1980.

Savizar and Silarra. *Light Speed: An Extraterrestrial Visionary Vehicle*. Earth Mission Publishing. 1990.

Savizar and Silarra. *Conscious Channeling: An Extraterrestrial Approach*. Earth Mission Publishing. 1989.

Savizar and Silarra. *The Awakening: Co-creating Heaven on Earth with Extraterrestrial Walk-ins*. Earth Mission Publishing. 1989.

www.ingramcontent.com/pod-product-compliance
Lightning Source LLC
Chambersburg PA
CBHW060317050426
42449CB00011B/2518